The American Crisis Series
Books on the Civil War Era

Steven E. Woodworth, Associate Profess
Texas Christian University
SERIES EDITOR

D0711073

 The Civil War was the crisis of the Republic's first century—the test, in Abraham Lincoln's words, of whether any free government could long endure. It touched with fire the hearts of a generation, and its story has fired the imaginations of every generation since. This series offers to students of the Civil War, either those continuing or those just beginning their exciting journey into the past, concise overviews of important persons, events, and themes in that remarkable period of America's history.

Volumes Published

James L. Abrahamson. *The Men of Secession and Civil War, 1859–1861* (2000). Cloth ISBN 0-8420-2818-8   Paper ISBN 0-8420-2819-6

Robert G. Tanner. *Retreat to Victory? Confederate Strategy Reconsidered* (2001). Cloth ISBN 0-8420-2881-1   Paper ISBN 0-8420-2882-X

Stephen Davis. *Atlanta Will Fall: Sherman, Joe Johnston, and the Yankee Heavy Battalions* (2001). Cloth ISBN 0-8420-2787-4 Paper ISBN 0-8420-2788-2

Paul Ashdown and Edward Caudill. *The Mosby Myth: A Confederate Hero in Life and Legend* (2002). Cloth ISBN 0-8420-2928-1 Paper ISBN 0-8420-2929-X

Spencer C. Tucker. *A Short History of the Civil War at Sea* (2002). Cloth ISBN 0-8420-2867-6   Paper ISBN 0-8420-2868-4

Richard Bruce Winders. *Crisis in the Southwest: The United States, Mexico, and the Struggle over Texas* (2002). Cloth ISBN 0-8420-2800-5 Paper ISBN 0-8420-2801-3

Ethan S. Rafuse. *A Single Grand Victory: The First Campaign and Battle of Manassas* (2002). Cloth ISBN 0-8420-2875-7 Paper ISBN 0-8420-2876-5

John G. Selby. *Virginians at War: The Civil War Experiences of Seven Young Confederates* (2002). Cloth ISBN 0-8420-5054-X Paper ISBN 0-8420-5055-8

Edward K. Spann. *Gotham at War: New York City, 1860–1865* (2002). Cloth ISBN 0-8420-5056-6 Paper ISBN 0-8420-5057-4

Crisis in
the Southwest

Crisis in the Southwest

The United States, Mexico, and the Struggle over Texas

The American Crisis Series

BOOKS ON THE CIVIL WAR ERA

NO. 6

Richard Bruce Winders

A Scholarly Resources Inc. Imprint
Wilmington, Delaware

Scholarly Resources
104 Greenhill Avenue
Wilmington, DE 19805-1897
www.scholarly.com

Library of Congress Cataloging-in-Publication Data

Winders, Richard Bruce, 1953–
    Crisis in the Southwest : the United States, Mexico, and the
    struggle over Texas / Richard Bruce Winders.
        p. cm. — (The American crisis series ; no. 6)
    Includes bibliographical references and index.
    ISBN 0-8420-2800-5 (alk. paper)—ISBN 0-8420-2801-3 (pbk. : alk.
paper)
    1. Texas—History—To 1846.   2. Texas—History—1846–1950.
3. United States—Relations—Mexico.   4. Mexico—Relations—
United States.   5. United States—Foreign relations—1815–
1861.   6. United States—Boundaries—Mexico.   7. Mexico—
Boundaries—United States.   I. Title.   II. Series.

F390.W77 2002
976.4'03—dc21   2001049151

∞ The paper used in this publication meets the minimum require-
ments of the American National Standard for permanence of paper
for printed library materials, Z39.48, 1984.

*With Sharon's concurrence, this book is dedicated
to our feline companions:*

*Carlos Gato de Béxar,
Catarina Dulce,
and Grey Cat—the one who came before.*

A Cat's Poem: A Stroll across the Keyboard

\ ]]]]
Za12QW
SaaaaZZ
Ppppppppppppppppppppppp9-..
                              Carlos

About the Author

Richard Bruce Winders is a recognized authority on U.S.–Mexican relations during the first half of the nineteenth century. *Mr. Polk's Army: The American Military Experience in the Mexican War* received the Jerry Coffey Memorial Book Prize for the best work in the field of military history for 1997. He served as assistant editor on *The United States and Mexico at War: Nineteenth-Century Expansionism and Conflict*, an encyclopedia project for Macmillan (1998). He has developed educational programs and material designed to assist teachers and students. A biography for juvenile readers, *The Life and Times of David Crockett, Frontier Legend*, is forthcoming. Awarded his doctorate in U.S. history from Texas Christian University, Winders has held the position of historian and curator at the Alamo since 1996.

Contents

INTRODUCTION

The proper name for the people of Texas seems to be
a matter of doubt or contrariety: some calling them
Texians, while others speak or write Texans, Texonians,
Texasians, Texicans. We believe that, both by the
Mexican and American residents of the country, the
name commonly used is Texians; the Mexicans giving
it the guttural sound of the Spanish language, as
indicated sometimes by *x* and sometimes *j*, Teghians.
The sound is not used in the present mode of speaking
the English language, although the Irish use it in the
word *lough*, and the Scotch in *loch*, a lake. The nearest
approximation is in such words as *Ch*rist.

Texians is, therefore, the correct name of the people
of Texas; and besides being short, it is perfectly
analogous to the usual mode of forming the proper
name of nations by the termination in *n*; It may also be
considered the euphonious abbreviation of Texasian.
But Texonian and Texasite are absurd epithets. *New
Orleans Bee.*
—*Telegraph and Texas Register*
November 7, 1835

IT IS HARD to imagine the course of U.S. history without Texas. More
than just a geographical space, Texas reflected the westward migration of Americans as they left the confines of their nesting grounds
along the Atlantic Coast and the trans-Appalachian region. It is also
hard to imagine the course of Mexican history, too, without Texas.
A northern borderland, Texas represented both security and potential prosperity to the young nation of Mexico. Although historians
often discount the notion of inevitability, a retrospective look at
Texas in first half of the nineteenth century seems to indicate that the
United States and Mexico were destined for conflict over control of
the region.

Continuity in history exists but often is missed by students and
the public. The problem partly stems from the way in which history
is taught. Textbooks, which are poor tools for learning history, are

arranged in chronological order and divided into chapters and units according to universally accepted benchmarks. The implication is that each new chapter represents a clean break from the past and is somehow a self-contained historical episode. This notion is so obviously erroneous that its mention seems almost ludicrous. Nevertheless, my experience has convinced me that the arbitrary periodization of history might be one of the greatest obstacles to our understanding of the past and, by extension, of ourselves.

The study of Texas and its role in early-nineteenth-century history suffers from this overemphasis on periodization. Texas writers have tended to concentrate on several apparently distinct episodes in the region's history: colonization (usually as related to the coming revolution), the Texas Revolution, and the Republic of Texas. Only a few writers have carried the story through to the Mexican War.

Texas and its role in early-nineteenth-century history also suffers from a provincialism that places Texas and Texans at the center of all historical events that affected the state and its inhabitants during this period. Developments in Texas were greatly shaped by people and events in both Mexico, with which Texas shares a border, and the U.S. Southwest. Hence, to understand Texas history fully one must view it through the broad lens of historical context provided by an awareness of both U.S. and Mexican history.

There is no shortage of studies on Texas, U.S., or Mexican history. As previously noted, most such studies have dealt with narrow issues that do not convey the concept of continuity. The present study is designed to highlight the link between events in Texas, the United States, and Mexico from 1821 through 1850. This choice of time frame is not intended to suggest that continuity does not exist prior to or after these dates but merely that I, too, must follow the dictates of periodization that I criticize. I hope that readers will realize that other connections can be made and will seek to make them on their own.

Historical continuity exists in several facets. One is geography. Like a giant game board, historical events occur and reoccur over the same landscape. A second source of historical continuity is provided by the people who participate in different events. Not unlike heroes, villains, and extras in a series of movie sequels, historical figures appear and reappear in subsequent historical episodes. Ideology forms the third leg of historical continuity. Disputes over basic ideological questions are never resolved permanently, providing a foundation for the seemingly never-ending battles between competing factions.

The geography of this story is continental in scope. The epicenter for the region is Texas, which by modern definition stretches from the Red River to the Rio Grande and from the Sabine River to the border of New Mexico. During the years examined in this study, however, Texas's borders contracted and expanded according to the dictates of the government that controlled the region at any given time. Thus, the reader of this work must clear from his or her mind the familiar image of the state established in 1850 and recognized today as Texas. In addition, much of this story occurs in the United States and Mexican nations. Again, one must make mental adjustments regarding the boundaries of these two nations. After the Missouri Compromise in 1820, the United States consisted of twenty-two states (eleven that banned slavery and eleven that permitted the institution) and the territory left over from the Louisiana Purchase. Mexico, organized into a federal republic after securing its independence from Spain, consisted of eighteen states and territories that included Upper and Lower California as well as New Mexico. The actual area of operation for the various military campaigns that occurred from 1835 to 1850 comprised nearly all of Mexico as defined in the Mexican Constitution of 1824.

An examination of studies on the Texas Revolution, the Texas Republic, and the Mexican War reveal that participants in one event often took part in at least one other event. Of Americans and Texans, one can point to such men as Sam Houston, Mirabeau B. Lamar, Edward Burleson, José Antonio Navarro, Thomas Jefferson Green, Hugh McLeod, John C. Hays, and Samuel H. Walker as examples. Mexican participants are also abundant, among them Antonio López de Santa Anna, Valentín Gómez Farías, José María Tornel y Mendivil, José Antonio Mexía, José Urrea, Pedro de Ampudia, Mariano Arista, and Antonio Canales Rosillo. Although we like to draw clear distinctions between opposing factions, this era took on the characteristics of a true civil war, causing its participants to make difficult choices and sometimes to pursue courses of action that differed widely from their original objectives. For instance, such persons as

José María Jesús Carbajal and Juan N. Seguín changed allegiances midway through the conflict.

Ideology permeates the writings from the Mexican War period, flowing from the pens of all participants regardless of nationality. The predominant concern was a timeless question, not confined to the participants' time and place: What is the nature of government and which form is best? Many American participants were the sons and grandsons of revolutionaries, reared in households in which reminiscences of the struggle for American independence were commonly heard. Mexicans also knew about revolution: Many had experienced it firsthand during the tumultuous years from 1810 through 1821. Radicals, among whom were Americans and Mexicans, championed the federal republic as the system of government most suitable for free men. Conservatives, a group also made up of American and Mexican supporters, favored limiting the power of the various states, reserving for the national government the power to make important decisions. An interesting irony resides in the terms used to label proponents of the federal republic: In the United States, they are called "anti-federalists," whereas in Mexican history they are called "federalists." Hence, Alexander Hamilton and Lorenzo de Zavala, whose respective positions in government were diametrically opposed, are both considered to be federalists.

U.S. proponents of concentrating power in the hands of the national government were not easily labeled, whereas Mexicans who worked for that goal were called "centralists." Opponents of Andrew Jackson had no qualms about calling "Old Hickory" (as he was known) a tyrant for his almost dictatorial use of his office; the same appellation applied to Santa Anna after he became a centralist.

Another ever-present ideological issue was secession, or the right of one part of a republic to voluntarily withdraw from the rest of the national union. Thus, there is an ideological link between events as seemingly diverse as the Texas Revolution, the founding of the Republic of the Rio Grande, and the American Civil War.

This book requires that the reader approach it with a willingness to see history in a different way. The study of history should not be confined by national borders or other arbitrary conventions imposed by historians, politicians, or the readers themselves. My goal is to help the reader to see old stories in a new light and to realize that each new crisis rises phoenixlike out of the ashes of the past.

TERMINOLOGY

Language is ever changing. Although creating and accepting new words is an important part of human growth, historians should take care to preserve the vocabulary of the periods with which they work. For this reason, I have chosen to use the older form of some words—"Monterey" and "Vera Cruz," for example. San Antonio often is called by its older name, "Béxar." I also have chosen to designate the Anglo participants in this work as "Americans," even though I realize that the same appellation can be applied to Canadians, Mexicans, and all other inhabitants of this hemisphere. Its usage in this historical context is clear. Although the term "U.S.–Mexican War" has gained wide acceptance, I prefer to retain use of the terms "Mexican War" and "Invasión de 1847," depending on the point of view to be reflected. Likewise, I find that the word "Texian" often confuses people, and so I use "Texan" instead. To avoid the use of "*sic*," all the quotations used in this book are preserved unchanged, regardless of misspellings, incorrect punctuation, and the like.

ACKNOWLEDGMENTS

Several individuals who provided assistance in the writing of this book deserve to be recognized. Daughters of the Republic of Texas Alamo Committee Chair Mary Carmack and Alamo Director Brad Breuer encouraged the project and understood its importance. Series editor Dr. Steven Woodworth, Texas Christian University, offered me the opportunity to be a part of the American Crisis Series. Scholarly Resources' Matthew Hershey provided guidance throughout the project. Thanks to both of these men for allowing me to present my interpretation, which goes beyond the accepted standard. André Csihas read the text for errors and provided valuable feedback. And, as always, I must thank my wife, Sharon, for her support and patience. Thanks, too, to all those who contributed to this work in ways that neither they nor I even realize.

List of Maps

CHRONOLOGY

1803	Louisiana Purchase places United States on the border of Spanish Texas
1810	Independence movement in Mexico begins with Father Hidalgo's revolt
1811	Royalists suppress republican "Las Casas Revolt"
1812	Republican filibusters led by Gutiérrez and Magee invade Texas
1813	Royalists crush republican forces at the Battle of Medina
1817	American filibusters under Henry Perry defeated near Goliad
1819	American filibustering expedition under James Long fails United States forfeits Texas's claim to Spain in Adams-Onís Treaty
1820	Revolt in Spain raises conservative concerns in Mexico U.S. Congress enacts Missouri Compromise Spanish officials in Mexico invite American colonists to Texas Missouri traders open trade with New Mexico, beginning Santa Fe Trail
1821	Mexico declares its independence from Spain Mexico proceeds with plan to colonize Texas
1823	Mexico adopts republican form of government Stephen F. Austin and others receive *empresario* contracts

1824	Mexican Federal Constitution of 1824 is adopted
	Texas joined with Coahuila to form Coahuila y Tejas

1826	*Empresario* Hayden Edwards stages unsuccessful revolt against Mexico

1829	A centralist coup replaces President Vicente Guerrero's administration

1830	Mexico cracks down on immigration from the United States

1832	Antonio López de Santa Anna backs federalist counterrevolution
	Andrew Jackson threatens to use force to end Nullification Crisis
	Anticentralist disturbances occur in Texas at Anahuac and Velasco

1835	War between federalists and centralists erupts in Mexico
	Texans join revolt against central government

1836	Texas declares its independence from Mexico and forms the Republic of Texas
	Sam Houston elected president of the Republic of Texas

1837	United States officially recognizes the Republic of Texas

1838	France invades Mexico in the Pastry War
	Texans spoil plans by Mexican agents to foster Indian uprisings
	Mirabeau B. Lamar elected president of the Republic of Texas

1839	French sign treaty with Mexico and evacuate Vera Cruz
	Federalists revolt against the central government and count on Texas's support

1846   War erupts between United States and Mexico
        U.S. troops occupy northern Mexico, New Mex-
            ico, and California

1847   Polk shifts U.S. war efforts to central Mexico
        U.S. troops capture Mexico City

1848   United States and Mexico sign Treaty of
            Guadalupe Hidalgo
        Gold discovered in California

1849   Gold rush boosts California's population, mak-
            ing early statehood possible

1850   Texas's modern state boundary determined by
            the Compromise of 1850

1861   Texas secedes from the Union
        Texas attempts to reestablish boundaries of the
            former republic

Cast of Characters

AMERICANS AND TEXANS

John C. Hays (1817–1883)

Although arriving in Texas too late to participate in the revolution, John C. Hays went on to become one of the Republic of Texas's most noted military chieftains. He first gained notice for his fights with the Comanche, leading his Texas Rangers against these fierce nomadic raiders. Slight of stature and plain-spoken, Jack Hays served with distinction under both Zachary Taylor and Winfield Scott in their campaigns in northern and central Mexico.

Sam Houston (1793–1863)

Flamboyant and headstrong, Sam Houston made an impression wherever he went. His bravery at the Battle of Horseshoe Bend in 1814 caught the attention of his commanding general, Andrew Jackson. Some suspected that Old Hickory later sent Houston to Texas to engineer its separation from Mexico. Although the conspiracy theory is questionable, undoubtedly the history of Texas would have been very different without Sam Houston.

John C. Hays

Sam Houston

Andrew Jackson (1767–1845)

General, planter, and politician, so important was Andrew Jackson to the development of the early United States that some writers have labeled the 1820s–1840s as the Age of Jackson. U.S. president at the time of the Texas Revolution, Old Hickory had already offered to purchase the region in question from Mexico. Two of his political protégés—Sam Houston and James K. Polk—developed into influential leaders, cast in the mold of their mentor.

George Wilkins Kendall (1809–1867)

Few contemporaries of George W. Kendall, who was neither politician nor soldier, had as great an effect on the national scene regarding Texas as did this co-owner and editor of *The New Orleans Picayune*. Taken prisoner in New Mexico while traveling with the Santa Fe Pioneers, Kendall later chronicled his experiences for his readers. Once war between the United States and Mexico commenced, Kendall, through his newspaper, reported the war firsthand to an awaiting American public.

Mirabeau Buonaparte Lamar (1789–1859)

Poet, politician, and editor, Mirabeau B. Lamar won the respect of his adopted countrymen in a skirmish with Mexican troops near San Jacinto. The transplanted Georgian, who served as Texas's second president, epitomized the promise of the Republic of Texas better than did any of his contemporaries. A Calhoun Democrat and foe of Andrew Jackson, Lamar and Sam Houston were destined to become bitter political enemies.

José Antonio Navarro (1795–1871)

A native of San Antonio de Béxar, José Antonio Navarro had blood ties to the influential Ruiz and Veramendi families. In 1813, Navarro had to flee to Louisiana after supporting the failed attempt to establish a republic in Texas. He later supported the Texans in their revolt against Mexico and signed the Texas Declaration of Independence. A member of the Texas Congress, he accompanied the Santa Fe Pioneers to New Mexico, where he was captured and sent to prison in Mexico. Escaping in 1845, Navarro returned to Texas in time to support the annexation movement.

James Knox Polk

Winfield Scott

James Knox Polk (1795–1849)

Although relatively unknown to most Americans, James K. Polk arguably had more influence on U.S. history than many other men who have occupied the White House. Vowing to serve for only one term if elected president, Polk set out to expand his country's borders even if it required war with Mexico. Known as "Young Hickory," he ruled his mentor's Democratic Party through intimidation and patronage. Despite the successful outcome of the war, Polk ended his term bitter and disillusioned, his party mortally wounded from the political battles it had fought.

Winfield Scott (1786–1866)

Few American military chieftains can match the achievements of Winfield Scott. Entering the War of 1812 as a captain, Scott ended the conflict as one of the army's senior ranking generals. Contentious and arrogant to a fault, Scott earned the sobriquet "Old Fuss and Feathers" because of his love of martial pomp and finery. Still, Scott was the premiere military mind of his day, a fact borne out by his spectacular capture of Mexico City.

Juan Nepomuceno Seguín (1806–1890)

Son of an influential San Antonio de Béxar family, Juan N. Seguín and his relatives opposed the abrogation of Mexico's Constitution of 1824. During the Texas Revolution, Seguín commanded a company of Tejanos at Béxar and San Jacinto. Although a close friend of many older Texans, his post-revolution success created hard feelings among newcomers, who conspired to drive him from Texas. Relocating to Mexico, Seguín served in the Mexican Army during Woll's Invasion in 1842 and the Mexican War.

Zachary Taylor (1784–1850)

Zachary Taylor had already won national acclaim for his 1837 victory over the Seminole Indians in Florida at the Battle of Ockeechobee. Commander of the military district that included Texas, Taylor drew the assignment of guarding the newly annexed state as commander of the Army of Occupation. Called "Old Rough and Ready" because of his lack of pretentiousness and his willingness to fight, Taylor traded the battlefield for the White House in 1848.

Zachary Taylor

Nicholas Philip Trist   Samuel Hamilton Walker

Nicholas Philip Trist (1800–1874)

A protégé of Thomas Jefferson and career diplomat, Nicholas P. Trist
seemed the perfect choice to represent the United States at the peace table.
Trist surprised his superiors, President James K. Polk and Secretary of War
William L. Marcy, by ignoring orders for his recall from Mexico. Despite
the controversy surrounding his actions, Trist constructed a peace treaty that
satisfied Polk's war aims.

Samuel Hamilton Walker (1817–1847)

A veteran of the Seminole War, Samuel H. Walker immigrated to Texas and
later participated in the Mier Expedition. He served in John C. Hays's company of Texas Rangers after escaping from captivity in Mexico. His daring
earned him a captain's commission in the U.S. Mounted Rifles. Only thirty
years old when killed at Huamantla, Mexico, Walker had become one of the
army's best-loved and most known officers.

MEXICANS

Lucas Alamán y Escalada (1792–1853)

Lucas Alamán witnessed the violence of mob action firsthand when Father Hidalgo's peasant army sacked Guanajuato and murdered the city's Spanish residents. The event forever turned him against populist movements and convinced him that Mexico needed the stability that only a strong central authority could provide. He became one of the Mexican conservative faction's most important and respected intellectual spokesmen. Not opposed to the establishment of a Mexican monarchy, Alamán looked to Europe for assistance against U.S. expansionism.

Pedro de Ampudia (1805–1868)

Cuban by birth, Pedro de Ampudia arrived in Mexico in 1821 amidst the last days of Spanish rule; he was active as a lieutenant in the royalist army. Choosing to remain in Mexico after independence, he received a commission in the Mexican Army. Serving in the Texas Campaign, Ampudia rose to a position of command in northern Mexico, where his forces battled Mexican and Texas federalist forces during the late 1830s and early 1840s. Ampudia had become one of Mexico's highest-ranking generals by the commencement of the Mexican War.

Lucas Alamán y Escalada   Pedro de Ampudia

Mariano Arista

Mariano Arista (1802–1855)

Like many of his contemporaries, Mariano Arista served as a young man in Mexico's war for independence under the charismatic Agustín de Iturbide. Early in his career, Arista displayed conservative leanings, supporting the Plan de Cuernavaca that gave Antonio López de Santa Anna a mandate to dismantle the federal republic. Reputed to be an expert on military matters, Arista was given the task of driving Zachary Taylor's Army of Occupation from the Rio Grande. Removed from command after the defeats at Palo Alto and Resaca de la Palma, Arista campaigned to clear his name and restore his tarnished reputation.

Antonio Canales Rosillo (1802–1869)

A lawyer and surveyor by trade, Antonio Canales Rosillo gained influence among his neighbors at Camargo on the Rio Grande. He supported the formation of the federalist Republic of the Rio Grande until the movement was crushed. By 1840 he had become a trusted ally of Mariano Arista and Pedro de Ampudia, leading local forces against incursions by Texans. Working with José Urrea, he commanded guerrilla operations in northern Mexico during the Mexican War.

José María Jesús Carbajal (?–1874)

Although a native of San Antonio de Béxar, as a young man José María Jesús Carbajal lived for a time in Kentucky and Virginia. Returning to Texas after embracing the Protestant religion, he worked for Martín de León and even married the *empresario*'s daughter. He supported the federalist cause in the Texas Revolution, later participating in the attempt to establish the Republic of the Rio Grande. Carbajal commanded irregular troops against the U.S. Army in northern Mexico during the Mexican War.

Valentín Gómez Farías (1781–1857)

Although trained as a physician, Valentín Gómez Farías twice served as vice president of Mexico, both times under Antonio López de Santa Anna. Unlike Santa Anna, however, Gómez Farías remained true to his ideology. A radical liberal, he supported policies that, if successful, would have altered Mexican society by lessening the power of the Catholic Church and the army. Gómez Farías pushed for war with the United States and opposed the Treaty of Guadalupe Hidalgo.

José Antonio Mexía (ca. 1800–1839)

Although the early details of his life are disputed, José Antonio Mexía fought for independence in Mexico's struggle to break free from Spanish rule. An ardent federalist, Mexía supported Antonio López de Santa Anna's overthrow of President Anastasio Bustamante's centralist regime in 1832. Four years later Mexía was fighting against his former ally by supporting the insurgents in Texas. Ever opposed to centralism, Mexía was captured in 1839 and executed by Santa Anna for participating in a federalist revolt.

Antonio López de Santa Anna (1794–1876)

From 1821 to 1854, Antonio López de Santa Anna so dominated Mexican politics that the period might be called the Age of Santa Anna. Although best remembered as the general who defeated the Texans at the Battle of the Alamo in 1836, this native of the Mexican state of Vera Cruz entered and exited the office of presidency more than ten times before finally falling into disfavor as a result of the Gadsden Purchase. The key to his success was his ability to adapt his political ideology to suit the mood of his nation. Called both an enigma and an eagle, Santa Anna is linked to the histories of three nations—Mexico, Texas, and the United States.

José Antonio Mexía   Antonio López de Santa Anna

José María Tornel y Mendivil (1789–1853)

Antonio López de Santa Anna relied on his supporters—Santanistas—
to keep him in office. One of his most powerful disciples was José María
Tornel, who worked behind the scenes to implement his chief's policies.
Tornel, who served as minister to the United States from 1829 through
1831, developed an intense dislike and fear of Mexico's aggressive neighbor to the north. The infamous Tornel Decree, issued while he was serving
as secretary of the army and navy, resulted in a series of mass executions
during the Texas Revolution.

José Urrea (1797–1849)

In an army characterized by mediocrity, José Urrea gained a reputation as
an energetic and able commander. During the Texas Revolution, Urrea's
victories over the insurgents in the Goliad area blunted the proposed Matamoros Expedition and handed the Texan-American force some of its most
serious defeats. Following the failed Texas campaign, Urrea joined forces
with federalist general José Antonio Mexía in an attempt to overthrow
the centralist government. Captured and offered clemency, Urrea oversaw
Mexican guerrilla operations in northern Mexico during the Mexican War.

ILLUSTRATION CREDITS

John Frost, *Pictorial History of Mexico and the Mexican War* (Richmond: Harrold and Murray, 1848): Pedro de Ampudia, 196; José Antonio Mexía, 171; Antonio López de Santa Anna, 361; John C. Hays, 294; James Knox Polk, 333; Winfield Scott, 577; Zachary Taylor, 358; Nicholas Philip Trist, 542; Samuel Hamilton Walker, 607.

The Life of Sam Houston (New York: J. C. Derby, 1855): Sam Houston, frontispiece.

Fayette Robinson, *Mexico and Her Military Chieftains* (Hartford: Silas Andrus and Son, 1851): Lucas Alamán Escalada, 267; Mariano Arista, 253.

CHAPTER ONE

SETTING THE STAGE FOR CRISIS
Colonization and Revolution

Those who have volunteered to join the Texonians, and
those who may wish to do so, are requested to meet the
committee at the Arcade this evening at six o'clock, for
the purpose of taking measures to organize themselves,
preparatory to an immediate departure; arms and
ammunition will be furnished them, and their passage
paid as far as Natchitoches.
—Notice to Volunteers
New Orleans, October 15, 1835

SPAIN FACED A serious problem in 1819: How could its northern borderlands be protected to ensure that they would remain Spanish? The missions and presidios that dotted the landscape from California's Pacific Coast to Louisiana's Arroyo Hondo had failed to draw enough inhabitants into the northern tier of New Spain to establish a secure claim. Russian trappers occupied strategic sites in northern California. Missouri business adventurers were on the verge of establishing regular trade over the Santa Fe Trail, which would economically annex Chihuahua and New Mexico to the United States. Fierce bands of nomadic raiders frequently swept across Texas, deterring settlers from the interior of Mexico who might otherwise have moved to the region. Texas seemed especially vulnerable as a steady stream of citizens from the United States began to spill westward, emboldened by the outcome of the War of 1812, which removed the British and Indians, who had formed an obstacle to growth.

Spain had already encountered aggressive Americans in Louisiana and Florida. Uncertainty over navigation rights on the Mississippi River and the right of deposit at New Orleans had led to the extraordinary purchase of the Louisiana Territory from France in

1

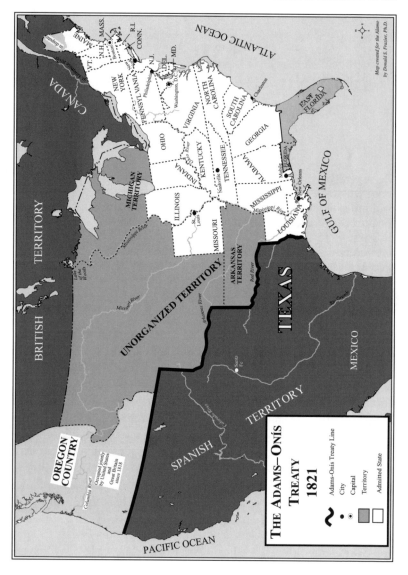

THE ADAMS–ONÍS TREATY 1821

Adams-Onís Treaty Line
City
Capital
Territory
Admitted State

1803, a development that suddenly placed Americans on the border of Texas. The terms of the purchase guaranteed future conflicts because the exact extent of the area remained undefined. Americans in the Old Southwest claimed that portions of Florida were included in the transaction and established U.S.-style republics there to lay claim to the region. U.S. troops under General Andrew Jackson invaded Spanish Florida in both 1816 and 1818, the first time to disperse a community of runaway slaves and the second to apprehend and execute two British citizens known to be aiding the southern tribes in their fight against American settlers. Realizing its hold on Florida and Texas was tenuous, Spain entered into negotiations with the United States over the future of these two possessions. In the 1819 Adams-Onís Treaty (also known as the Transcontinental Treaty), Spain renounced all rights to West and East Florida in exchange for the United States assumption of $5 million in claims made against Spain by American citizens and the clear delineation of Texas's border with the United States. The Sabine River was designated as a boundary with Louisiana to the east and the Red River created a boundary with Arkansas Territory to the north, so that, for the moment, Spanish Texas seemed safe.

Nevertheless, Spanish officials were concerned that Texas's sparse population left the region open to encroachment. Spain needed a loyal population on which it could depend to ward off invasion from both nomadic tribes and the United States. Colonization appeared to be the answer.

Moses Austin achieved a special place in history as the man who opened Texas to settlement by Americans. Born in Connecticut in 1761, Austin followed a circuitous path to Texas. He and a brother obtained a contract to roof the Virginia state capitol in 1789. The venture sparked an interest in lead, a metal used in roofing and other trades. He soon developed a lead mining and smelting business and, later in 1789, moved his operations to Missouri, then under Spanish control. (Spain, which wanted to increase the population of its North American territories, had invited men such as Austin to settle. Many Americans accepted the offer, including famed frontiersman Daniel Boone.) Austin acquired controlling interest in lead deposits at Mine à Burton near the modern town of Potosi and soon established his firm as the foremost lead producer in the region. However, the fortune he amassed ebbed away during the tumultuous years surrounding the War of 1812, and efforts to reverse his losses through land speculation in Arkansas Territory failed. When the Panic of 1819 struck, Austin decided the time had arrived to pursue new opportunities, and Spanish Texas beckoned.

Moses Austin traveled to San Antonio de Béxar in 1820 to discuss with Spanish authorities his plan to bring colonists to Texas. Governor Antonio María Martínez, however, was uninterested, and Austin may never have assumed his historic role had it not been for a chance encounter with an old acquaintance. Felipe Enrique Neri, better known as Baron de Bastrop, had come to know Austin in New Orleans years earlier, and the two men recognized each other when they met on the streets of Béxar. Bastrop, who had moved to Texas after the Louisiana Purchase, was a longtime resident of San Antonio and a friend of the governor. He interceded on Austin's behalf and helped to convince Martínez to endorse Austin's plan to colonize Texas. Austin returned to Missouri to recruit colonists and there learned that Martínez's superiors also had granted approval of the plan. However, like Moses of Biblical times, Austin was not destined to enter his promised land. The journey from Texas in midwinter took its toll on Austin's health. His deathbed request was that his son, Stephen Fuller Austin, fulfill the plan of taking American colonists to Spanish Texas.[1]

Although only twenty-eight years old at the time of his father's death, Stephen F. Austin already had gained valuable experience that would aid him in his new role as *empresario,* or land agent. Born in Virginia, the younger Austin had spent two years at Kentucky's prestigious Transylvania University before helping to run his father's mining and smelting enterprise. On the public front, he had served as both a member of the Missouri territorial legislature and an officer of the state militia before moving to Natchitoches, Louisiana, where he studied law. It was there that he learned of the elder Austin's death. Although not eager to abandon his own plans, Stephen F. Austin readily assumed his father's place as the colonizer of Texas.

On Austin's arrival in Texas in the summer of 1821, Governor Martínez acknowledged him as the legitimate heir to Moses Austin's grant. Officials allowed Austin to explore freely to select a site for his colony. He chose a fertile area east of San Antonio that was watered by the Colorado and Brazos Rivers and included Matagorda and Galveston Bays. His contract called for him to settle 300 families on this land. Each married man was to receive up to 4,428 acres for himself as well as additional amounts of land for each family member or slave. For serving as administrator of the colony, Austin would charge twelve cents per each acre he assigned, to cover his expenses. As *empresario*, he would also be awarded substantial amounts of land for his own use. After consulting with Martínez, Austin returned to the United States to promote his colony.

The newly commissioned *empresario* had no trouble finding Americans who were interested in relocating to Texas. The same economic depression that had convinced Moses Austin to request a land grant in Spanish Texas created a ready pool of prospective colonists. Land meant livelihood to people living in an agrarian society. With public land in the United States selling for $1.25 per acre, the 12-cents-per-acre administrative fee paid to Austin was an offer too attractive to pass up. Colonists were enlisted quickly and began arriving in Texas in early 1822. With more recruits on the way, Austin returned to Texas to oversee the establishment of his colony.

However, this time Austin would not be dealing with Spanish officials: Despite its efforts, Spain had finally lost its grip on its North American possession. On September 27, 1821, Colonel Agustín de Iturbide marched into Mexico City at the head of an insurgent army, effectively ending Spain's 300-year reign over Mexico. Independence movements had gained momentum in Latin America after Napoleon Bonaparte imprisoned King Ferdinand VII and placed his own brother, Joseph Bonaparte, on the Spanish throne. Revolt against Spain first erupted in Mexico on the night of September 16, 1810, when peasants answered the call for independence issued by Father Miguel Hidalgo y Costilla at the small village of Dolores. Although Hidalgo's army soon was crushed and the priest captured and executed, rebels and royalists battled one another for the next ten years. Restored to the throne in 1814, Ferdinand alienated his liberal supporters by reversing reforms that had been instituted in his absence. In 1820 liberal army officers in Spain staged a revolt that resulted in reinstatement of the Spanish Constitution of 1812. By 1821, Mexican royalists and rebels both were ready to sever ties with Madrid. The uniting of these old enemies to prevent the spread of radical changes promised by the junta spelled disaster for New Spain. Mexico was now on its own and free to chart its own course.

In compliance with Governor Martínez's instructions, Austin traveled to Mexico City to confer with the new government regarding the confirmation of his *empresario* contract. He arrived at the end of April 1822 to find a chaotic situation resulting from the birth of a new nation. The revolution had upheld three important principles: independence from Spain, protection of the Catholic religion, and equality among all Mexicans. Its leaders intended to establish a Mexican monarchy and hoped to place a European nobleman on the newly created throne. When no such nobleman accepted the offer, Iturbide orchestrated a barracks revolt, after which, on May 19, 1822, the Mexican Congress agreed to crown Iturbide as Mexico's first constitutional emperor. It was into this tumultuous milieu that Austin stepped.

The colonization issue occupied much of the new Mexican Congress's attention. Other Americans approached officials about land grants. New colonization laws finally were enacted, and Austin's contract was confirmed. After a year-long stay in Mexico City, Austin left for Texas. The delay of his departure, however, worked to Austin's benefit, because it allowed him to learn the language and culture of his adopted home. The courteous and sincere manner with which he conducted himself made a favorable impression on Mexican authorities, and Austin left Mexico having formed valuable friendships with influential members of the new government.

The situation in the Mexican capital continued to change in ways that would affect Texas. Mexico's first attempt at self-government ended in failure when popular opinion, backed by the army, forced Iturbide to resign as emperor on March 19, 1823, and to leave the country. Various factions within Mexico had been vying with one another to shape the new government to their liking. The contenders in this power struggle were monarchists, centralists, and republicans. The first two groups shared similar constituencies and goals but differed as regards the means by which they intended to accomplish their objectives. Both the monarchist and centralist groups were composed of the most powerful segments of Mexican society: the military, the church, and owners of large estates. Whereas monarchists were willing to serve either a foreign- or a native-born king on the throne of Mexico, centralists were more progressive and ready to jettison the monarchy. To centralists, a republic built around a strong central government appeared to be what Mexico needed. To both groups, however, preserving the status quo in society by recreating the institutions of the Spanish period was all-important. Most affected by the Enlightenment were Mexico's liberals, who, like their American counterparts Patrick Henry and Thomas Jefferson, were convinced of the virtues of a federal republic. The intense struggle between these factions rocked Mexico for decades, the shock waves being felt in every corner of the emerging nation.[2]

Beginning in 1823 Mexican federalists allied themselves with centralists to institute a republican-style government. The experiment lasted until federalist reforms outstripped public desire for change and the centralists gained ascendancy. Among the most notable accomplishments of the federal Republic of Mexico was the adoption of the Mexican Constitution of 1824. When drawing up this important document, its authors consulted both the U.S. Constitution and the Spanish Constitution of 1812.[3] Mexico's adoption of a federal system of government offering constitutional guarantees to its citizens was attractive and comforting to American colonists in Texas.

Austin's colony prospered under his leadership. From his headquarters at San Felipe de Austin, Austin dispensed titles and advised his colonists to be good Mexican citizens. Changing citizenship and accepting the Catholic faith were considered by the colonists to be small concessions for acquiring land on which to build their futures.[4] By the end of 1824, Austin had settled 300 families in his colony, fulfilling his obligation to the government. He requested and received subsequent contracts.

Austin, however, was not the only *empresario* in Texas. While Austin was in the capital securing his own contract, Mexico City had been teeming with applicants for grants. Nearly twenty individuals of various nationalities were awarded contracts by the Mexican government. Green DeWitt, a Missourian (as was Moses Austin), received a grant for land adjacent to the southwest boundary of Austin's colony. Martín de León, a Mexican national, obtained a grant that placed him along the southwest boundary of Austin's colony. Confusion over the border between DeWitt's and de León's land proved to be a continual source of friction between these two *empresarios.* Lorenzo de Zavala, who had helped to author the federal Constitution of 1824 and held the position of governor for the state of Mexico, was another Mexican national who received a grant. Mexican military personnel were encouraged to participate in colonization. Vicente Filisola, an Italian-born general serving in the Mexican Army, secured permission to establish a colony. Another Mexican officer, Martín Perfecto de Cos, also received a contract to settle Mexicans in Texas. Other prominent *empresarios* included Robert Leftwich, Benjamin Rush Milam, Hayden Edwards, Sterling C. Robertson, Gaspar Flores, Joseph Vehlein, David G. Burnet, James Powers, John McMullin, and James McGloin.

Despite the initial success of *empresarios* such as Austin, DeWitt, and de León, misunderstandings and abuse placed the entire colonization system in jeopardy. That American and Mexican ideas of land ownership were dissimilar soon revealed itself as a fundamental difference between the two cultures. Reared in the Spanish land tradition, in which all land ultimately belonged to the king, Mexican society viewed a land grant as a right to occupy and use assigned land legally, a concept that implied a close and continuing relationship between the state and the recipient. Americans, on the other hand, believed strongly in the ownership of private property, such that land, once it had been acquired, could not be taken away without due process. Persons in the United States were operating under a serious misconception—namely, that land in Mexico was for sale. Although many settlers registered with *empresarios* and became legal colonists, an increasing number crossed the border independently from Louisiana to look for land. The situation was further confused by the fact that several *empresarios* sought investors and organized corporations for the purpose of speculating in Texas lands. Other *empresarios* defaulted on their contracts when they were unable to entice settlers to take advantage of their land grants. As a result of these infractions and failures, some Mexican officials who had supported colonization began to wonder whether they had made a mistake.

Hayden Edwards created the first serious clash between an *empresario* and the Mexican government. On April 14, 1825, Edwards had received permission to settle colonists in the area of Nacogdoches. The land he was granted was home already to many people, who had built houses and cultivated fields there. Edwards and his supporters ignored the concerns of these residents and threatened to evict them unless the residents could prove that they had a valid claim to the land they occupied. The established settlers turned out to oppose the election of Edwards's son-in-law as *alcalde* (mayor), but the *empresario* declared his daughter's husband the winner anyway. Mexican officials investigated claims of election irregularities and found that many supporters of the Edwards faction had voted illegally. Thus, the election was overturned, and officials eventually revoked Hayden Edwards's *empresario* contract.

Nonetheless, Edwards and his supporters refused to leave. On December 21, 1826, they gathered at the Old Stone Fort in Nacogdoches and announced the formation of the Freedonia Republic, basing their action on the principles of independence, liberty, and justice. Although the Freedonians hoped to enlist the Cherokee and other northeast Texas Indians in their cause, no such alliance was consummated. Mexican officials sent troops to put down the revolt, and Edwards and his followers fled across the border into Louisiana. Stephen F. Austin, as commander of his colony's militia, mobilized his colonists in support of the Mexican government and marched to Nacogdoches to help restore order. Despite Austin's display of loyalty, Mexican officials remained concerned: How many other colonists, like Edwards, harbored dreams of independence?

Worries were heightened by the findings of Mexican officers sent to Texas to investigate the situation. Manuel de Mier y Terán, a Mexican general who conducted a survey of Texas for his government, arrived in 1828 and found that American settlers outnumbered native Mexicans ten to one in the area where the *empresario* contracts had been filled. The situation was dire: Texas was being overrun by Americans. Xenophobia had already surfaced in the nascent republic, as evidenced by Mexico's expulsion of Spaniards from its borders in 1827. It may not have been possible to expel the Americans, but something had to be done to stem their flow into Mexico.

In reaction to Mier y Terán's report, the government passed a series of measures designed to assert its control over Texas. Tax exemptions granted to stimulate colonization were not renewed, and tax collectors were appointed to oversee the establishment of customhouses. Regulations against importing slaves were to be enforced. The construction of new military posts and the reinforcement of existing garrisons by convict soldiers were ordered. Even more drastic, a decree known as the Law of April 6, 1830, banned colonization from the United States and encouraged European immigration.[5] Another officer, Juan Almonte, traveled through Texas in 1834 to follow up on Mier y Terán's findings and the changes that resulted from implementation of the Law of April 6. Almonte contended that "the Anglo-American settlers are influenced by self-interest and not patriotism."[6] These actions were made possible because the centralist faction had gained control of the government, and curtailing the power of the states was the centralists' prime objective.

Mexican politics had entered a tumultuous period. The republic's first elected president, insurgent hero Guadalupe Victoria, would be the only man to complete his term of office for the next forty years. Even so, in 1827 he had to crush a revolt against his government led by his own vice president, Nicolás Bravo. The presidential election of 1828 pitted conservative Manuel Gómez Pedraza against Vicente Guerrero, a liberal general and hero of the wars for independence. Although Pedraza won the contest, Guerrero and his supporters refused to recognize the election results. Several of Guerrero's fellow generals, including Antonio López de Santa Anna, staged barracks revolts against President Pedraza. Liberals in Mexico City engineered a popular uprising in favor of Guerrero in which rioters looted the shops of foreign merchants in the city's Parián Market. By April 1829 continuing unrest forced Pedraza into exile, and Guerrero assumed the mantle of the presidency.

Guerrero and his followers had begun a vicious cycle that Mexico would come to regret. Fewer than nine months later, Guerrero faced troubles of his own. A liberal, he had used his office to abolish slavery and to expel Spanish citizens from Mexico. The last action resulted in a Spanish military expedition against Tampico, which was defeated by a combination of coastal diseases and an army commanded by Mier y Terán and Santa Anna. In the aftermath of the invasion, conservatives led by Vice President Anastasio Bustamante revolted against Guerrero, who refused to relinquish extralegal powers that were granted to him by the Mexican Congress so that he could deal with the Spanish threat. The conservatives claimed that they were acting to uphold the constitution, and the Mexican Congress removed the president and replaced him with Bustamante.

Guerrero, who remained in the field at the head of troops loyal to him, finally was captured and, on February 14, 1831, was executed by a firing squad. The death of Guerrero turned many Mexicans against Bustamante. Santa Anna pronounced against the conservative president and led his army to Mexico City, entering the capital on January 3, 1833. Bustamante went into exile, and Pedraza was recalled to serve the last three months of his term, as if that gesture would somehow restore Mexico's political health. On April 1, 1833, Santa Anna was elected to serve his first of many terms of office.

Events in 1832 in Texas had also been tumultuous. A dispute over import taxes, runaway slaves, and issues of self-government arose between the military commander at Anahuac and the American colonists at the nearby town of Liberty. In June 1832, Colonel Juan Davis Bradburn, a Kentuckian in service of the centralist government, arrested local attorneys William B. Travis and Patrick C. Jack for promoting antigovernment activities. Friends of the two men came to their aid, forming armed companies and demanding the release of Travis and Jack. A skirmish at Velasco resulted in casualties on both sides and centralist evacuation of the fort there. The situation was brought under control by the arrival of General José Antonio Mexía, Bradburn's superior, who was convinced by the colonists that the disturbance was part of the federalist counterrevolution led by General Santa Anna against President Bustamante. Travis and Jack were released, and military garrisons were reduced or, in some places, eliminated altogether.

The Turtle Bayou Resolutions, adopted on June 13, 1832, presented a defense of the colonists' actions while simultaneously setting forth the colonists' political philosophy. The document read in part:

> Resolved. That we view with the deepest feelings of regret, the manner in which the Gover't of the Republic of Mexico is administered by the present [centralist] dynasty—The repeated violations of the constitution—the total disregard of the law—the entire prostration of civil authority; and the substitution in the stead of a military despotism, are grievances of such character, as to arouse the feelings of every freeman, and impel him to resist.
> Resolved. That we view with feelings of the deepest interest and solicitude, the firm and manly resistance, which is made by

the highly talented and distinguished Chieftain—General Santa
Anna, to the numberless Incroachments and infractions, which
have been made by the present administration, upon the constitution and law of our adopted and beloved county.
    Resolved. That as freemen devoted to a correct interpretation,
and enforcement of the Constitution, and laws, according to their
true Spirit—We pledge our lives and fortunes in support of the
same, and of the distinguished leader [Santa Anna], who is now so
gallantly fighting in defence of Civil Liberty.[7]

Although such talk might easily be dismissed as pure political rhetoric, one must keep in mind that these are the same people about
whom General Mier y Terán, on his trip through Texas only a few
years earlier, wrote, "They all go about with their constitution in
their pocket, demanding their rights and the authorities and func-
tionaries that [it] provides."[8] Although he probably was speaking
figuratively, Mier y Terán clearly understood that the American settlers were sticklers for their rights as they viewed them and were
more than ready to defend those rights when challenged.
    The colonists endeavored to resolve their grievances through
less militant means. In October 1832 delegates met at San Felipe de
Austin to ask the government to renew tax exemptions, to repeal the
Law of April 6 and, generally, to grant more local rule. The boldest
measure called for Texas to be politically split from Coahuila and
formed into a separate state within the Mexican Federation. Austin
cautioned that the time was not yet right to present these demands
because no native-born delegates attended the meeting and the document would therefore be perceived as an attempt on the part of
ungrateful American colonists to cause trouble. In April 1833, however, delegates reconvened and revived their demands. The new
convention appointed Austin to carry its petition to Mexico City.
    Although Austin's mission started well, things soon went horri-
bly wrong for him. Meeting with influential members of the Mexican Congress once he arrived in July, he was able to have the Law of
April 6 modified to allow for a resumption of colonization from the
United States. He made little progress, however, on the other issues.
Leaving Mexico City in December, a discouraged Austin penned a
letter to friends in Texas, telling them to proceed with the plan for
separate statehood even though the national government had not
granted permission for them to do so. The imprudent message fell
into unfriendly hands, and Austin was arrested by officials at Sal-

tillo and returned to Mexico City, where he spent the next year in prison. On his release from confinement in December 1834, Austin was refused permission by the government to leave the capital until the following July. By then, gone were his words of conciliation, replaced with the warning, "The federal constitution of 1824 is about to be destroyed, the system changed, and a central or consolidated one established."[9]

Austin's absence from Texas created a power vacuum. His supporters counseled restraint, not wishing to make matters worse for the imprisoned Austin. But with Austin away, more radical elements came to the forefront. In July 1835 trouble again erupted at Anahuac, where Travis and a small band of colonists captured the garrison in a dispute brought on by the arrival of a new tax collector. Although he expected his actions to be approved, Travis found that many colonists thought he had behaved rashly and actually condemned the attack. News of the impending arrival of Martín Perfecto de Cos with reinforcements for Béxar and other garrisons, however, provided an issue around which the colonists could unite. Travis promised Texans that they would not be alone, writing, "News from New Orleans that we will be liberally aided with men, money, and arms, has arrived."[10] A call went out for a new meeting, designated the Consultation, to be held at San Felipe in October.

Events moved quickly now. Federalist revolts had erupted throughout Mexico. The popular and charismatic Santa Anna, who had rallied to the aid of federalists in 1832, had become president in 1833. After his election, he withdrew to his estate, Manga de Clavo, near Vera Cruz and allowed Vice President Valentín Gómez Farías to implement reforms that threatened the power of the church and army. If these changes were carried out, Mexican society itself would be restructured. Conservative elements demanded that Santa Anna must resume his office and reverse the reforms. Santa Anna returned to Mexico City and resumed his presidential authority under the Plan de Cuernavaca, which granted him extraordinary legal powers to deal with the current situation.

To the dismay of the federalists who had earlier supported him, Santa Anna began dismantling Gómez Farías's reforms. He dismissed Mexico's national congress, which was meeting in special session, allowing his supporters to reconvene a congress composed of centralists. The Plan de Cuernavaca called for abandonment of the federal system in favor of a centralized government and for the conversion of the separate states into departments run by officials appointed by Mexico City. The new Mexican Congress was authorized to write a new constitution that reflected the change in government being implemented.

Civic militias belonging to the states were viewed as a threat to the dominance of the national army and were ordered reduced. Control over state governments that resisted these assaults on the federal system had to be imposed if the rising tide of centralism was to succeed. In May 1835, Santa Anna led an army to Zacatecas, where he and his lieutenant, Martín Perfecto de Cos, routed Governor Francisco Garcia's militia forces and then sacked the capital city.[11]

Federalist sentiment also boiled up in Tamaulipas and Yucatán. The situation in Texas, however, demanded immediate attention if it were to be saved. After the July 1835 disturbance at Anahuac, Mexican troops again headed to Texas to reinforce its military garrison and prepare for an upcoming campaign designed to nip the rebellion in the bud by seizing militants such as William B. Travis and the exiled federalist leader Lorenzo de Zavala.[12]

Much of Texas's growing rift with Mexico had its roots in the unwieldy marriage of Texas to Coahuila, imposed after independence. According to the initial arrangement prescribed by the Mexican Congress and the federal Constitution of 1824, Texas—because of its sparse population—was to be treated as a department within the state of Coahuila and Texas. Although the name implied equality, the lion's share of the political power rested with the governing faction at Saltillo, the state's capital. The state legislature was composed of eleven representatives from several municipalities: three representatives from Saltillo, three from Monclova, three from Parras, one from Guerrero, and one from Béxar. Set against the backdrop of the struggle between the federalists and centralists for national power, events in Coahuila and Texas revealed another struggle—one between regional factions for political and economic dominance.[13]

Saltillo had been the traditional seat of authority for the region during Spanish rule. Political power translated into economic power as well. The municipality's elite expected to continue Saltillo's leadership role in the Mexican Republic. On September 6, 1830, José María de Letona of Saltillo was elected governor. After a short delay, Juan Martín de Veramendi, a successful merchant from Béxar, was installed as lieutenant governor. Veramendi had close ties to many American colonists in Texas, including his famous son-in-law, James Bowie.

The death of Governor Letona on October 14, 1832, set in motion a series of events that ultimately led to civil war. As expected, Veramendi assumed the office of governor. An outsider to the Saltillo junta, Veramendi gained the support of two powerful brothers from Parras, José María and Augustín Viesca. José María Viesca held the post of governor from 1828 through 1831 and served as president of the executive council. Wishing to break the hold Saltillo held over the region, Veramendi, Viesca, and the majority of the state legislature backed a plan to move the capital to Monclova. The bill passed on March 9, 1833, with only the representatives from Saltillo voting against it. Thus, the capital of Coahuila and Texas was changed officially to Monclova, a shift greatly resented in Saltillo.

The legislature and the governor relocated to Monclova, but the anti-Saltillo faction suffered a severe blow when, in September 1833, a cholera epidemic ravaged the town, claiming Governor Veramendi and his family. With both the governor and lieutenant governor deceased, José María Viesca filled the post until, on January 8, 1834, the legislature appointed a new governor, Francisco Vidaurri y Villaseñor.

The Monclova faction continued to chip away at Saltillo's power base. On March 18, 1834, the governor approved legislation that divided Texas into three departments—Béxar, Brazos, and Nacogdoches—and allotted each a legislative seat, thereby increasing the number of anti-Saltillo representatives.

Pleased with its newly acquired power, the Monclova faction made the fateful step of meddling in national politics. On June 24, 1834, with the legislature out of session, the caretaker legislative council proclaimed its support for the federalists and announced that it viewed all acts of Santa Anna as illegal because of his dismissal of Mexico's national congress on May 31, 1834. Several days later the legislative council passed two additional resolutions: Coahuila and Texas would not permit any national troops within the state nor would it reduce the size of the state's militia.

The Saltillo junta now had grounds to resist the Monclova faction. Its representatives sided with the centralists and named José María Goribar as the state's governor. Both sides fielded their respective militias. Dr. James Grant, an *empresario* who held land grants near Parras, was named to command the federalist troops. Although no pitched battles were fought, minor clashes occurred around Saltillo.

The political situation remained fluid. Vidaurri y Villaseñor stepped down as governor of the strife-torn state and was replaced by Juan José Elguézabal. In September 1834, General Martín Perfecto de Cos was appointed commandant of the Eastern Internal Provinces, a military district that included Tamaulipas, Nuevo Léon, and Coahuila and Texas. With close ties to Santa Anna, Cos vowed to uphold the authority of the government in Mexico City. The Monclova faction continued to pursue its own course when, in the following month, it held a special session in which it elected Augustín Viesca as governor.

In December 1834, Santa Anna offered a compromise solution to the impasse: In a gesture recognizing the anti-Saltillo faction's concerns, Monclova was permitted to remain the state capital. Elguézabal would continue to serve as governor until new elections could be held. To rid the region of political partisans, especially those not loyal to him, Santa Anna directed that no one who had previously served in the state legislature or on the executive council could be a candidate in the upcoming election. The move would prevent the Monclova faction's leadership from participating in the new legislature or holding any other state offices.

The new election, as ordered by Elguézabal, was held in January 1835. The rebellious departments and municipalities failed to obey Santa Anna's directive and returned their former representatives to office. The legislature met at Saltillo on March 1, 1835, at which time Elguézabal submitted his resignation and the legislature appointed José María Cantu of Monclova as his replacement until a new election for governor could be held. Clearly still out of power, the three representatives from Saltillo quit in protest.

The regional dispute was about to enter its final stage. On March 14, 1835, Cantu declared Saltillo in revolt and called out the militia to quell the insurrection. On March 20, 1835, Augustín Viesca was sworn in as newly elected governor, in violation of Santa Anna's directions that no one who had held office before be selected. Because the state's treasury was nearly empty, Viesca and the legislature decided to sell unsettled tracts of land in Texas to raise money to finance the state's defense. Cos and other supporters of the government in Mexico City pointed out that the plan violated the spirit, if not the letter, of the nation's and state's colonization laws and was thus unlawful.[14]

As commander of the Eastern Internal Provinces, Cos announced that he was sending troops to Monclova to monitor the situation. He had learned that the radical federalist Gómez Farías, recently deposed as vice president, had been staying with Viesca. Cos believed that he and other disgruntled federalist leaders such as Lorenzo de Zavala and José Antonio Mexía intended to use Texas as a base of operation against the centralists. The revolt in Zacatecas diverted his attention from Monclova, as Santa Anna needed him and his army first to suppress the Zacatecans.

Viesca arrived at Monclova on April 14, 1835, and was inaugurated as governor the next day. Within a week, he increased the likelihood of bloodshed by asking the various departments to send their militias to Monclova to help defend his new administration. Texas was one of the few departments to respond. His supporters included James Bowie, Dr. James Grant, Frank W. Johnson, Benjamin Rush Milam, Samuel M. Williams, and other prominent American colonists. Powerful Tejano families, including the Seguíns and Navarros, also supported Viesca. On May 21, 1835, Viesca named Béxar the new capital in order to distance himself from his enemies as well as to seek the safety of a friendlier political climate.

On June 5, 1835, Viesca and his party were arrested as they tried to reach Texas. He and the other captives were held at Monterey throughout the summer. The escape of one of the governor's companions, Benjamin Rush Milam, prompted an order for the prisoners to be transferred to San Juan de Ulúa, an impregnable fortress at Vera Cruz from which escape would be nearly impossible. But on October 25, 1835, while the party was en route to Vera Cruz, the commander of Viesca's guard, Lieutenant Colonel José Maria Gonzales, unexpectedly revolted in favor of the federalists and set the governor free. The governor, Gonzales, and their followers then headed for Texas.

The revolt in Texas in the meantime had already erupted into a full-scale military conflict. In late summer 1835 news arrived that Cos was bringing troops with which to occupy Texas. The colonists were infuriated. Austin, recently returned from captivity in Mexico City, worked to bolster resistance, telling the San Felipe Committee of Public Safety, "WAR is our only resource—there is no other remedy but to defend our rights, our country and ourselves by force of arms."[15] Responded John W. Moore to Austin, "All to a man in this quarter are preparing for the defence of their country against military tyranny and despotism. Texas & Liberty is the motto."[16] In September the colonists at Gonzales learned that Mexican troops intended to reclaim a small cannon given to the town for protection against marauding Indians. Although the gun had no real use other than to make noise, it quickly became a symbol, conjuring up images for the American-born settlers of the British march on Lexington and Concord in 1775. A flag appeared among the Texan ranks that bore the likeness of a cannon and the words "Come and Take It." On the morning of October 2, 1835, the colonists and soldiers exchanged shots. Unable to retrieve the cannon, the detachment rode away, reportedly leaving at least one of their number dead on the ground. Flushed with victory over their success in this small skirmish, the colonists planned to keep the initiative by taking the fight to the centralists. They scored another victory in the early morning hours of October 9 when armed colonists—joined by Benjamin Rush Milam—surprised and, after a brief struggle, captured the garrison at Presidio La Bahía (Goliad). The momentum, for the time being, clearly lay with the colonists. Word was dispatched for all Texans to turn out, "armed and equipped for war even to the knife."[17]

The colonists' response to these events was consistent with the frontier military tradition. A crisis was at hand, and men willing and able to bear arms put down their axes, hoes, and plows and picked up their muskets and rifles. This hasty gathering of colonists was designated the Army of the People and, true to the democratic nature of such expeditions, the men elected a leader, bestowing the title of general on Austin. Leading what amounted to a collection of independent commands, Austin set course for San Antonio de Béxar, where General Cos had arrived on October 9 with reinforcements to bolster the centralist forces in Texas.

Cos announced his arrival at Béxar in an address to his soldiers that left no doubt that a heavy hand was about to fall on Texas:

> The veil which has long concealed the perfidious designs of the colonists is at length withdrawn. These ungrateful men have revolted against our government, assumed the right to live as they like, without any subjection to the laws of the republic. They are presumptuous enough to believe that the nation which has

adopted them as her sons, has no sufficient power to subdue them and compel them to share that obedience to which they have sworn.[18]

In rallying his troops to the ordeal that faced them, Cos revealed his feelings and that of his government about the American colonists who had settled in Texas.

On arriving outside Béxar, Austin began probing Cos's defenses for weaknesses, prompting the Mexican general to react. On October 28, colonists under the command of James Bowie and James W. Fannin withstood an attack near Mission Concepción just south of Béxar, adding to the rebels' string of victories. Explained the two commanders in their official report, "Evry man was a soldier and did his duty agreeable to the circumstance and situation in which he was placed."[19] Although the victory emboldened the Texans and men continued to flock to Béxar, the Army of the People began to show signs of strain as the siege dragged on and colder weather arrived.

In addition to forming an army, the Texans also went about the task of creating a government. Delegates gathered at San Felipe for the Consultation that had previously been called in response to the summer disturbance at Anahuac. By now the situation was far more serious, as fighting between the colonists and the government troops had actually broken out. Before adjourning on November 14, the delegates accomplished several important tasks, including (1) authorizing the creation of a regular army under the command of Sam Houston; (2) issuing a *Declaration of Causes* that stated the rebellion had been brought on by the centralists' abrogation of the federal system; and (3) deciding to send commissioners to the United States to obtain support for the Texan cause. The first of these actions created a paper army that gave the dangerous and erroneous illusion that the Texans actually had a bona fide military force. The second reached out to Mexican federalists, both in and out of Texas, in the hope that a united front could be formed against Santa Anna. The third action acknowledged that the Texans needed men, money, and supplies if they were to succeed and that their kinsmen in the United States could be persuaded to provide this aid. Additionally, the Consultation formalized a provisional wartime government with an executive in the form of a governor—Henry Smith of Brazoria—and a legislative body, the General Council.[20]

At Béxar the siege dragged on. The Texans achieved yet another victory when, in an incident called the Grass Fight, they intercepted a pack train carrying forage for Cos's horses. The Texans outside Béxar learned that the Consultation had named Austin one of the commissioners to go to the United States. Command of the army fell to Edward Burleson. With winter coming and the town still not taken, many of the colonists began to drift away, returning home to tend to their families. Their action revealed the underlying weakness of the frontier military tradition, which dealt effectively with short-term emergencies but failed miserably when troops had to be kept in the field for long periods.

Indecision gripped the Texans gathered at Béxar. Some wanted to attack the town immediately, while others wanted to go into winter quarters and resume the campaign in the spring. Benjamin Rush Milam, then with the army at Béxar, rallied the remaining Texans for an assault on Cos's garrison. Early on the morning of December 5, 1835, the Texans slipped down the streets toward the main plaza and gained a foothold in town. Fighting hand-to-hand and room-to-room, the Texans steadily pushed the garrison back. On the fifth day of the battle, Cos surrendered the town. In capitulating, the Mexican general accepted a parole for himself and his army after he promised to withdraw his troops to the Rio Grande and to offer no further opposition to the "reestablishment of the federal constitution of 1824."[21] Another Texan victory had been won.

Events outside Texas had developed that would shape the direction and conduct of the revolution in the coming months. Help from abroad had begun to materialize even before the Consultation turned to the United States for assistance. In October, Texan sympathizers in New Orleans raised two companies of volunteers (the New Orleans Greys) and sent them to Béxar.[22] The arrival of these companies proved instrumental in carrying out the attack on the centralist garrison.

New Orleans spawned another expedition in October, one led by former Santa Anna supporter General José Antonio Mexía, then in exile for his opposition to the centralist government. He and other exiled liberals had prepared a plan to overthrow Santa Anna and install a new federalist government, relying on Texas to support their effort. Mexía, Gómez Farías, and Lorenzo de Zavala were to be the leaders of the new regime. Each first had a specific task to perform: Zavala was to work with colonists in Texas, Mexía was to seize Tampico as a base of operations for the federalists, and Gómez Farías was to oversee the plan in general. Mexía recruited volunteers for a planned federalist uprising in the state of Tamaulipas and sailed for Mexico. After landing at Tampico, however, he learned that the revolt there had already been crushed and that centralist forces knew of his coming. Mexía managed to escape with part of his expedition after a disorganized attack on the city, but more than thirty of his men were captured and brought to trial. Although the prisoners claimed that they were actually colonists bound for Texas and not revolutionaries, Mexican authorities declared them "pirates" and ordered their execution. This tragic and little-known affair had far-reaching effects.[23]

The united front for which the Consultation had hoped failed to develop. In November the governor of the state of Coahuila and Texas, Agustín Viesca, accompanied by his new ally, Lieutenant Colonel Gonzales, appeared at Goliad. To his dismay, he found that the Texans refused to recognize his authority. In December the survivors of Mexía's ill-fated expedition landed in Texas, where the federalist general sought assistance to continue his campaign against Santa Anna. Surprised to receive little encouragement and, in some cases, encountering downright hostility, Mexía quit the field and returned to New Orleans. Some Texans were beginning to see all Mexicans, whether federalist or centralist, as the enemy.

A definite rift had developed among the Texans that was to have dire consequences. Governor Smith and the General Council held opposing views regarding the course of the revolt and refused to cooperate. Worse than gridlock, each labeled the other's actions illegal and began acting independently, pursuing contradictory courses. Smith ordered the Council to disband, which prompted the Council to vote to replace him with Lieutenant Governor James W. Robinson. In explaining the difficulty to a supporter, Smith wrote, "My council became basely corrupt. . . . I sent them the Devil in the form of an address. . . . They notified me that I was removed from office &c and a new Governor was made &c. I knew however that they could not break me to make a new one—and I could adjourn them by force, that is by cutting off all communications with them."[24] One can sense the confusion that the rift created in the correspondence of one Texan official, who wrote to Smith regarding supplies for the

Texas military forces: "Without pretending to determine who is the acting Govern. I have forward two exact copies one to James W. Robertson and this to your Excellency."[25] This lack of unity had serious consequences for the Texans when the Mexican Army returned to Texas.

Smith, an ally of Sam Houston, belonged to the proindependence faction that had voted against the Consultation's November 7 *Declaration of Causes*, while the majority of the General Council were supporters of Austin. Smith's faction was known as the War Party, owing to its willingness to fight. The opposing faction, called the Peace Party, desired to find less violent means by which to achieve its objectives. The Peace Party pushed for the alliance with other Mexican Federalists while the War Party was the first to express the desire to sever ties with Mexico and all Mexicans.

A plan had been proposed in late 1835 to launch a campaign to seize the port city of Matamoros located near the mouth of the Rio Grande. Originally, the object had been to coordinate with General Mexía in his effort to wrestle Tamaulipas from the centralists. Both Smith and the General Council remained convinced of the plan's merits even after Mexía's failure to capture Tampico. Smith ordered that the expedition be overseen by Houston, who in turn entrusted the task to his ally, James Bowie. The General Council appointed its own commander, Frank W. Johnson, who declined the offer. They then commissioned James W. Fannin to lead the expedition. When Johnson reconsidered and decided to claim his post, the General Council failed to revoke either Fannin's or Johnson's appointment, so that the expedition officially had three commanders, a situation guaranteed to create chaos.

Besides the Texan garrison that occupied Béxar after Cos's defeat, several semiautonomous military commands existed in Texas, the largest of these at Goliad. Located on the San Antonio River about 100 miles downstream from Béxar, Goliad became the focal point of the Matamoros Expedition. Promoters of the plan were Frank W. Johnson and Dr. James Grant, both of whom had been prominent in the dispute between Monclova and Saltillo. They convinced nearly 200 volunteers from the Béxar garrison to join them in the proposed advance on Matamoros. Before leaving, Johnson and Grant commandeered stockpiled provisions and clothing intended to support the men of the Béxar garrison through the winter. They also took a herd of horses, leaving Lieutenant Colonel James C. Neill, the post commander, without means to conduct scouting forays. Complained Neill to the government, "It will be appalling to you to learn . . . [of] our alarming weakness."[26] Houston tried to exert his influence over the growing collection of men at Goliad, but most refused to recognize his authority over them. Failing to gain control of the expedition, he left on furlough to treat with the Texas Cherokee. Fannin, elected the commander of the garrison at Goliad, organized his forces while Johnson and Grant advanced to the village of San Patricio to gather supplies and livestock, a move that put them beyond Fannin's direct control. With no unity of command, civil or military, the insurgents were unprepared for the centralists' response to the rebellion.

Cos's advance on Béxar in October 1835 had been intended as the vanguard of a military sweep through Texas. As Austin and his supporters had warned, the centralists viewed the uprising as an effort by ungrateful foreigners to sever territory from Mexico. Just days prior to the loss of Béxar, Santa Anna had ordered the army to rendezvous at San Luis Potosí. Gathering supplies and conscripts, he planned to return to Texas without waiting for spring. With the national treasury nearly empty, Santa Anna mortgaged part of his property and forced loans from the church and merchants to finance the campaign. By mid-December his army was organized; by late January, advanced elements had crossed the Rio Grande headed northward.

The campaign called for a 2-pronged march into Texas. One of Santa Anna's lieutenants, General José Urrea, marched his brigade to Matamoros to investigate rumors that Lieutenant Colonel Gonzales had stirred federalist activity along the lower Rio Grande. Once there, Urrea turned northward toward Goliad to confront the Matamoros Expedition. Santa Anna personally accompanied General Joaquín Ramírez y Sesma's division as it journeyed from Presidio del Rio Grande destined for Béxar. Both Mexican columns would follow divergent branches of the old *Camino Real*. Béxar and Goliad lay in their path. The rebel troops gathered at these two strategic points were about to pay for their infractions against Mexico's central government.

Santa Anna entered Béxar on February 23 and began a 13-day-long siege of the Texan garrison occupying a former Spanish mission known as the Alamo. Béxar's commander, Lieutenant Colonel Neill of the fledgling regular Texas Army, had left a week earlier on a short leave of absence, intending to return in about thirty days. Reflecting the split between volunteers and regulars, the volunteers refused to recognize the authority of Neill's temporary successor, Lieutenant Colonel Travis. A quick election had determined that Travis and James Bowie would share joint command of the garrison until Neill's return. Travis assumed total command of the garrison on the second day of the siege when Bowie fell ill and had to be confined to his quarters. The rebel garrison numbered somewhat more than 150 members, including former U.S. Congressman David Crockett of Tennessee. The garrison also included a small number of Béxar natives, Mexican federalists who opposed Santa Anna. Even though the Mexican Army slowly encircled the former mission over the next two weeks, Travis was able to send messengers through the enemy lines with poignant requests for aid. On March 1, a small contingent numbering thirty-two men from Gonzales made their way inside the fort. The siege ended on the morning of March 6, 1836, when Santa Anna launched a predawn assault against the Alamo and put the garrison to the sword.

The eastern prong of the centralist advance also made progress in combating the rebels. Urrea encountered isolated detachments belonging to Johnson and Grant's command at San Patricio (February 26) and Agua Dulce Creek (March 2) as he marched toward Goliad. At La Bahía, renamed Fort Defiance by the volunteers manning the post, Fannin received requests for aid from Travis. After starting toward Béxar with a relief force, news of Urrea's movements caused his officers to hold a council of war in which they decided to return to Goliad. Orders from General Houston instructed Fannin to evacuate Goliad and join him at Victoria. Reluctant to leave until a missing detachment returned, Fannin finally abandoned the old presidio on March 19. After a short march of several miles, Fannin halted his command on the prairie near Coleto Creek, disregarding the urging of some of his officers and men to continue on to the tree-lined bank that lay ahead. The centralist forces that had been trailing Fannin succeeded in trapping the Texans on the open plain. Both sides exchanged fire throughout the afternoon. The following morning Urrea received reinforcements, including artillery with which he could pound the entrenched Texans. Fannin, himself wounded, polled his command, the majority of whom voted to surrender to Urrea. By all appearances, the momentum had shifted, and the centralist forces, as in the case of Zacatecas, were making short work of the rebellion. One of the hallmarks of the Texas campaign was the brutality with which it was conducted. Santa Anna and his supporters believed that the revolt was not really a revolt at all but an invasion by foreigners intended to separate Texas from Mexico. After Mexía's failed Tampico expedition, Santa Anna had dispatched General Ramírez y Sesma to reinforce Cos at Béxar with the following instructions, issued on December 7, 1835: "The foreigners who wage war against the Mexican Nation have violated all laws and do not deserve any consideration, and for that reason, no quarter will be given them as the troops are to be notified at the proper time. They have audaciously declared a war of extermination to the Mexicans and should be treated in the same way."[27]

The Mexican Congress endorsed this course of action, which was formalized by José María Tornel, the Mexican minister of war, in a proclamation that bore his name. The Tornel Decree, issued on December 30, 1835, reaffirmed that "foreigners landing on the coast of the republic or invading its territory by land, armed with the intention of attacking our country, will be deemed pirates and dealt with as such."[28] Even though many officers in the Mexican Army disagreed with this policy, Santa Anna insisted that it be carried out to the letter of the law. The result was a series of mass executions in the wake of the centralist victories, which tainted the Mexican Army's successes. The largest of these incidents occurred on Palm Sunday (March 27) when more than 300 men under Fannin's command, who believed themselves prisoners of war because Urrea had accepted their surrender, were marched from the fort at Goliad and shot down by their guards. These acts guaranteed that the Texans would respond in kind when the opportunity arose.

Santa Anna and his centralist supporters were correct that the Texas rebels were receiving assistance from foreigners, aid that came predominantly from the United States. The agents selected by the Consultation to go to the United States crossed the country raising money, supplies, and men. Even without the prompting of Texas agents, the people of the United States stood ready to help their countrymen struggling in a foreign land. Volunteers stepped forward at rallies throughout the nation. Citizens in Cincinnati donated two cannon called the Twin Sisters. In addition to those from New Orleans, military companies were raised in Kentucky at Paducah, Bardstown, and Newport; in Mississippi at Natchez; in Georgia at Macon; and in Alabama at Mobile. Volunteers from the United States played a critical role in 1836, as colonists failed to return to the field in large numbers. In fact, many of the men killed at Béxar and most of those executed at Goliad were U.S. volunteers in the service of the Provisional Government of Texas. Following the storming of the Alamo on March 6, Santa Anna sent to Mexico City the captured flag of the New Orleans Greys, which bore the words "First Company of Texan Volunteers from New Orleans," as proof that "foreigners" were indeed fighting on Mexican soil.

Reflecting on Texas's future in the unrest created by Mexico's ongoing civil war between the federalists and centralists, Stephen F. Austin observed that "a gentle breeze shakes off a ripe peach."[29] A positive action that had come out of the Consultation was a call for a new convention to be held at the small town of Washington located on the Brazos River. Austin's prediction came to fruition when on March 2, 1836, the delegates formally split from Mexico after securing unanimous approval for a declaration of independence.

In attendance was Sam Houston, whose position as commander of the Texas Army was reconfirmed by the ad interim government and was even expanded to include all forces currently in the field, authority that had not been granted by the Consultation in October. On March 6, Houston left Washington for Gonzales where he planned to take charge of reinforcements for Béxar who had gathered there. Arriving on March 11, he found that news of the Alamo's fall had been received and the townspeople were greatly alarmed, as they feared that Santa Anna would soon be upon them. Hurriedly packing what could be carried on horse, wagon, or one's own back, the colonists began a dash toward Louisiana known as the Runaway Scrape. The panic proved infectious and quickly spread to other communities, so that families clogged the rain-drenched roads. Taking command of the troops gathered at Gonzales, Houston ordered a general retreat eastward, instructing Fannin to abandon Goliad and join him at Victoria. Intercepted on his way to Victoria by Urrea, Fannin and his command were defeated and captured. The Palm Sunday execution of Fannin's command left Houston with only the men under his direct command and any volunteers from the United

States who might join him later. Panic and despair gripped the Texans, as it looked likely that the centralists' war of extermination might succeed.

Success, however, had made Santa Anna overconfident and caused him to discount the fighting abilities of the Texans. Dividing his forces into three columns, Santa Anna advanced eastward, driving the colonists before him. Houston and his army steadily withdrew, refusing to make a stand. The newly formed Texas government also retreated. When Santa Anna learned that the revolution's officials, including his old foe Zavala, were at Harrisburg, he set off in pursuit with a small detachment, leaving it for the larger column to follow later. Unable to catch the members of the new government, who barely slipped away, Santa Anna was now overextended and vulnerable.

Houston had come under great criticism for not making a stand against Santa Anna immediately after assuming command of the Texan forces in March. During the retreat, dissatisfaction had grown to such a point that Houston's men openly defied his orders, and several companies refused to serve under his command. But by April 19, Houston had resolved to fight, writing to his future father-in-law:

> This morning we are in preparing to meet Santa Anna. It is the only chance of Saving Texas. From time to time I have looked for reinforcements in vain. The Convention adjourning to Harrisburg struck *panic* throughout the country. Texas could have started at least four thousand men. We will have only about seven hundred to march with, besides the camp guard. We go to conquer. It is wisdom growing out of necessity to meet the enemy now; every consideration enforces it. No previous occasion would justify it. The troops are in fine spirits, and now is the time for action.[30]

On April 21, 1836, the hunter became the prey when the Texan army attacked and defeated Santa Anna in a bend of the San Jacinto River near present-day Houston. Shouting "Remember the Alamo!" colonist and volunteer alike sought revenge for the victims of the Tornel Decree. The casualty list tells of the ferocity of the Texan attack—more than 630 Mexican soldiers killed and 730 captured as compared to nine Texans killed and thirty wounded. Two of the captured Mexicans were General Cos and Colonel Juan Almonte. The day after the battle, another important prisoner was brought in that made victory even sweeter. Texan scouts had found a Mexican soldier hiding in a canebreak, and he turned out to be Santa Anna. Although it was still too early to declare the war over, events had turned against Mexico in favor of the new Republic of Texas.[31]

The Texan victory at San Jacinto has often been interpreted as the end of the war between Mexico and its former territory. More correctly, it signified an end to the first stage of the conflict, but the independence struggle was not over. For nearly ten more years the Texas question would shape events on both sides of the Rio Grande.

NOTES

1. The story of Moses and Stephen F. Austin is well known. For biographical studies, see David B. Gracy II, *Moses Austin: His Life* (San Antonio: Trinity University Press, 1987); Eugene C. Barker, *Life of Stephen F. Austin: Founder of Texas, 1793–1836* (1926; Austin: University of Texas Press, 1969); and Gregg Cantrell, *Stephen F. Austin: Empresario of Texas* (New Haven: Yale University Press, 1999).

2. Studies of this important period of Mexican history include but are not limited to Timothy E. Anna, *Forging Mexico: 1821–1835* (Lincoln: University of Nebraska Press, 1999); Michael P. Costeloe, *La primera república federal de México, 1824–1835* (Mexico City: Fondo de Cultura Económica, 1975); and Stanley C. Green, *The Mexican Republic: The First Decade, 1823–1832* (Pittsburgh: University of Pittsburgh Press, 1987).

3. The text of the Mexican Constitution of 1824 appears in Mary Austin Holley, *Texas* (1836; Austin: Texas State Historical Association, 1990), 365–392.

4. Eugene C. Barker, "The Government of Austin's Colony, 1821–1831," *Southwestern Historical Quarterly* (January 1918), 223–252.

5. Alleine Howren, "Cause and Origins of the Decree of April 6, 1830," *Southwestern Historical Quarterly* (April 1913), 378–422.

6. Helen Willis Harris, "Almonte's Inspection of Texas in 1834," *Southwestern Historical Quarterly* (January 1938), 211.

7. *The Constitutional Advocate and Texas Public Advertiser* (Brazoria), September 12, 1832; and Charles A. Gulick Jr. and Katherine Elliot, eds., *The Papers of Mirabeau Buonaparte Lamar* (Austin: A. C. Baldwin, 1920–1927), 1:142–143.

8. Jack Jackson, ed., *Texas by Terán: The Diary Kept by General de Mier y Terán on His 1828 Inspection of Texas* (Austin: University of Texas Press, 2000), 100.

9. John H. Jenkins, ed., *The Papers of the Texas Revolution: 1835–1836* (Austin: Presidial Press, 1973), 1:426.

10. Ibid., 1:381.

11. Colonel A. A. Greene, ed., "The Battle of Zacatecas," *Texana* (fall 1969), 189–200.

12. Jenkins, ed., *The Papers of the Texas Revolution*, 1:292, 414; 2:17.

13. H. Yoakum, *History of Texas from its First Settlement in 1685 to its Annexation to the United States in 1846* (New York: Redfield, 1856), 1:322–326. Also see Richard M. Gaines, *The Federalist War in Coahuila y Texas, 1832–1835* (Gonzales, TX: Clements Creek Press, 1999).

14. Eugene C. Barker, "Land Speculation as a Cause of the Texas Revolution," *Quarterly of the Texas State Historical Association* (July 1906), 83–92.

15. Jenkins, ed. *The Papers of the Texas Revolution*, 1:472.

16. Ibid., 1:485.

17. Ibid., 2:16.

18. Ibid., 2:111.

19. William T. Austin, "Account of the Campaign of 1835 by William T. Austin, Aid to Gen. Stephen F. Austin and Gen. Edward Burleson," *Texana* (winter 1966), 310.

20. Eugene C. Barker, ed., "Journal of the Permanent Council, October 11–27, 1835," *Quarterly of the Texas State Historical Association* (April 1904), 249–278.

21. Jenkins, ed., *The Papers of the Texas Revolution*, 3:156.

22. Ibid., 2:115–117.

23. Jenkins, ed., *The Papers of the Texas Revolution*, 1:416–423; and Eugene C. Barker, "The Tampico Expedition," *Quarterly of the Texas State Historical Association* (January 1903), 169–186.

24. Jenkins, ed., *The Papers of the Texas Revolution*, 4:63–64.

25. Ibid., 4:243.

26. Ibid., 3:424.

27. Ibid., 3:114.

28. *Telegraph & Texas Register,* March 12, 1836; and *The Mexican Side of the Texan Revolution by the Chief Mexican Participants,* translated by Carlos E. Castañeda (1928; Washington, DC: Documentary Publications, 1971), 53–54. Oddly, *The Papers of the Texas Revolution*, 3:379, does not reprint the full text of this important document but instead contains only a one-sentence annotation. Several editions of *Mexican Side of the Texan Revolution* exist, and pagination varies.

29. Jenkins, ed., *The Papers of the Texas Revolution*, 1:360.

30. Amelia W. Williams and Eugene C. Barker, eds., *The Writings of Sam Houston, 1813–1863* (Austin: University of Texas Press, 1938–1943), 1:413.

31. For an account of the Mexican prisoners after the Battle of San Jacinto, see Margaret Swett Henson, "Politics and the Treatment of the Mexican Prisoners After the Battle of San Jacinto," *Southwestern Historical Quarterly* (October 1990), 189–230.

CHAPTER TWO

PRELUDE
Texas and Mexico at Odds

He [General Bravo] said to me: [The Texans] are not
American citizens, and you have, therefore, no right
to interpose in their behalf. I replied: They are human
beings and prisoners of war, and it is the right and
duty of all nations to see that Mexico does not violate
the principles and usages of civilized war—more
particularly is it the duty of the United States to
maintain those laws and usages on this Continent.
—Waddy Thompson, U.S. Minister to Mexico
Recollections of Mexico (1846)

GENERAL ANTONIO LÓPEZ DE SANTA ANNA, the president of the Republic of Mexico, was the prisoner of Texan insurgents. What would
be the fate of this man who had conducted a war of extermination to
reclaim Texas from the foreigners who occupied her? Calls for his
execution were immediate: Had he been found on the day of the
battle, no power on earth could have saved him from the wrath of
those who sought vengeance for San Patricio, Béxar, Refugio, and
Goliad. Apprehended the day after the battle, his captors failed to
recognize him until he had reached the safety of Houston's camp.
Once there, the Texan commander granted him protection pending
a decision on how to dispose of the important captive.

With the president of Mexico in their hands, officials of the ad
interim government realized that keeping Santa Anna alive might
be the surest way to secure Texas's independence. Houston and
Santa Anna had already agreed to an armistice in which the Mexican leader ordered his remaining armies in the field to halt their
advance. Texan officials now offered to make a strategic pact with
Santa Anna in exchange for his life. On May 14, 1836, under the direction of President David G. Burnet and Vice President Lorenzo de
Zavala, Santa Anna placed his signature on two documents known

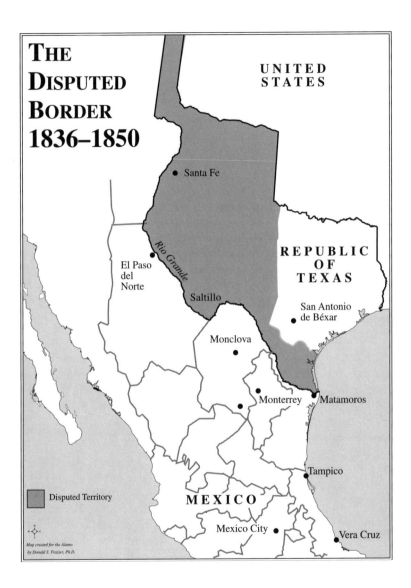

THE
DISPUTED
BORDER
1836–1850

UNITED
STATES

● Santa Fe

REPUBLIC
OF
TEXAS

Rio Grande

El Paso
del
Norte

Saltillo

San Antonio
● de Béxar

Monclova
●

Monterrey
●

● Matamoros

Tampico

Disputed Territory

MEXICO

Mexico City ●

Vera Cruz

Map created for the Alamo
by Donald S. Frazier, Ph.D.

collectively as the Treaty of Velasco. The first of these was a public accord in which Santa Anna promised (1) to cease his attempt to bring Texas under Mexican control; (2) to order an immediate cease-fire on both land and sea; (3) to order all Mexican troops in the field to withdraw south of the Rio Grande; (4) to order Mexican troops to respect all people and property they encountered during the evacuation; (5) to return all private property seized, including slaves and indentured servants; (6) to order his troops to avoid making contact with Texan forces; and (7) to order his troops to conduct their withdrawal with all possible speed. The public treaty also arranged for the exchange of prisoners, including Santa Anna, who was to be transported to Vera Cruz "as soon as it shall be deemed proper." The second treaty, to be kept secret by the captive Mexican leader and Texan officials, reiterated Santa Anna's promise not to take up arms against Texas again. Furthermore, it required Santa Anna to use his influence with his countrymen in securing recognition of Texas's independence and to promote Texas's commercial interest by lobbying for a trade treaty. Most important to future developments, the document indicated that the boundary between Texas and Mexico lay at the Rio Grande. In return for these guarantees, Texas officials promised to return Santa Anna to Mexico without delay.[1]

Even with this momentous turn of events, Texas remained in a chaotic state. Homesteads lay abandoned and fields went unplowed as colonists gathered along the Texas-Louisiana border in makeshift refugee camps. Crops needed to be planted and livestock tended, but the fear of renewed hostilities prevented settlers from immediately returning to their farms. To make matters worse, a raiding party composed of Comanche and Caddo struck Fort Parker on May 19, 1836, killing one man and carrying two women and three children into captivity. The attack fueled concern that a Mexican-backed Indian uprising was about to engulf the region. The raid also prompted General Edmund P. Gaines to order several companies of U.S. regulars from Fort Gibson, Indian Territory, to Nacogdoches, reportedly to prevent the hostilities from spilling over into Louisiana. His actions did little to ease Mexico's concerns over United States designs on Texas.

Many of the colonists who had served at San Jacinto left the ranks but, instead of shrinking, the size of the army actually mushroomed as fresh volunteers from the United States continued to arrive by the boatload. These men had answered the call for aid issued several months before, when Texas officials needed all the troops they could muster. Inspired by republican rhetoric and looking for land and adventure, these newcomers actually added to the chaos by refusing to take orders from the ad interim government. In June 1836 one such group of volunteers landed at the port of Velasco to discover that Santa Anna was on board the Texas warship *Invincible*, preparing for his return to Mexico as specified in the treaty. Led by Thomas Jefferson Green, a brigadier general in the Texas Army, the newly arrived volunteers demanded Santa Anna's continued imprisonment, if not his life, forcing President Burnet to agree to the Mexican president's protracted confinement to avoid his likely lynching by the mob. In another incident of mass insubordination, General Mirabeau Buonaparte Lamar resigned from the army after the troops in the field refused to recognize his appointment as commander of the Texas Army by President Burnet. Having overthrown one military despot, the citizens of the new republic faced the very real threat of a new military tyranny imposed by those who had come to rescue them.

Beset with a list of mounting problems, President Burnet decided to speed up the election for the permanent government in order to achieve stability for the new republic. On July 23, Burnet proclaimed September 5 as election day. The field of candidates included several well-known figures. Henry Smith, the provisional governor appointed by the Consultation, entered the race. While Stephen F. Austin seemed a likely choice, many of the newer arrivals to Texas distrusted him for his one-time pro-Mexican stance. As in other cases in history, the electorate clamored for a military hero, and General Sam Houston fit the bill. When the votes were tallied Austin had 587, Smith had 743, and Houston had 5,119. Lamar, who briefly had held the post of secretary of war and a general's commission in the Texas Army, was elected vice president. Both Austin and Smith received posts in the new administration, the former *empresario* as secretary of state and the former provisional governor as secretary of treasury. With Houston at the helm, the Republic of Texas prepared to follow the course to nationhood.

That course would be far from smooth. Mexican military forces withdrew below the Rio Grande but only to regroup. Many officers wished to continue the campaign while still on Texas soil, but the army became bogged down in the mud created by torrential spring rains, which made both roads and rivers impassable. General Vicente Filisola, who, as second in command, took over after Santa Anna's capture, had little choice but to break off the campaign and withdraw. Once the army was out of Texas, the Mexican government began preparations for the reconquest of Texas. In the summer of 1836 rumors of a new campaign spread throughout the new republic when Texas prisoners in Matamoros slipped a message hidden in a whip handle to authorities, warning of imminent invasion.

Problems, both internal and external, prevented an immediate return by the Mexican Army. Recriminations began while the withdrawal was barely under way, as various officers blamed one another for the disaster that had overtaken the Texas campaign. Santa Anna, still a prisoner in Texas, was quick to castigate his army for not properly supporting him at San Jacinto. Filisola blamed Urrea. Urrea blamed Filisola. Junior officers most often took the side of the general under whom they served. The government promised to investigate the matter as participants published partisan accounts of the campaign, defending their own conduct while excoriating their enemies. The hard feelings created by the mishandling of the campaign affected Mexican politics and events in Texas in the years that followed.

Santa Anna finally returned to Mexico on February 21, 1837. Texas authorities had been able to stave off calls for his execution by keeping him and his staff in seclusion. By late November 1836, Houston decided the time was right to send the Mexican leader home. Texas officials, however, chose a circuitous route for Santa Anna, taking him on what amounted to a tour through the United States that culminated in Washington, DC, where U.S. officials introduced him to Andrew Jackson. Back on Mexican soil, Santa Anna claimed that the Treaty of Velasco had been coerced and, even if it had not been, that the Texans had broken the agreement by prolonging his captivity. For the time being, Santa Anna retreated to his hacienda near Vera Cruz, as it was apparent that the magnitude of his misconduct overshadowed his charisma.

By 1838, Mexico faced crises on several fronts that were, for the moment, of a higher priority than chastising wayward Texas. In April 1838 a French fleet blockaded the port of Vera Cruz, a move prompted by Mexico's inability to pay damages claimed by French citizens against the Mexican government. Dubbed the Pastry War because of the charge that xenophobic participants of the 1828 anti-Spanish Parían Market riot had looted the shop of a French baker, the conflict meant that the Mexican military first had to expel the French before any campaign into Texas could be contemplated. In November, with diplomatic negotiations at a standstill, the French fleet bombarded Vera Cruz, an action condemned by governments around the world.

The Pastry War paved the way for a triumphal return to public life by Santa Anna. Leaving his estate, Santa Anna rushed to Vera Cruz and offered his services to the Mexican forces there fighting the French. A cannonball smashed his left leg, and doctors amputated the mangled limb just below the knee. For many of his countrymen during this trying time, this "sacrifice" redeemed Santa Anna's lost honor and restored him to the pantheon of Mexican heroes. Santa Anna not only recovered from his physical wound, but his political injuries also were healed. By 1839 he was again president of Mexico.

The Pastry War was not Mexico's only problem: Rebellion had broken out again in several of her states. Federalist sentiment remained high along the Rio Grande in the wake of the Texas Revolution, a feeling the local leaders built into outright opposition to the centralist regime. In 1838, Antonio Zapata, Antonio Canales, and others raised a revolt in the small town of Guerrero in the state of Coahuila. The following year federalist supporters revolted in Tampico. Mexican federalists counted on aid from Texas, and Texans rallied to their aid, drawn to the cause for a variety of reasons. Near Mier, federalists under General José María Jesús Carbajal, who were assisted by American volunteers defeated and nearly captured a larger centralist force. Buoyed by their successes, Canales established a federalist camp on the Nueces River to recruit more Texans. Canales even visited San Antonio to round up volunteers. In September 1839, Canales and his Texan allies recrossed the Rio Grande into Mexico. The following month, they defeated centralist forces at the Battle of Alcantro near Mier. In December, centralists in Matamoros resisted a federalist siege of the city. Many of the Texans left in disgust when Canales vetoed an attempt to take the city by storm. The federalist leader next marched to Monterrey, where he and centralist commander Mariano Arista clashed on Christmas Day. Canales, unable to deliver the blow needed to topple the centralists in northern Mexico, withdrew to the Rio Grande to replenish his supplies and reinforce his depleted ranks.

Centralist forces had scored a clear victory earlier in the year near Puebla in central Mexico. There the federalist leaders were José Urrea and José Antonio Mexía, two principal actors in the Texas Revolution. Urrea, whose troops had dealt such devastating blows in the area around Goliad, had joined with Mexía in revolt against their government. On April 30, 1839, government troops under Santa Anna clashed with the federalists at Puebla. Urrea, who narrowly escaped capture by centralist forces following this shattering defeat, renounced the federalist cause and was welcomed back into the government's fold. Mexía, who was not lucky enough to evade capture, was executed on Santa Anna's order owing to his long-running opposition to the centralists. When informed that his former ally had allowed him time to prepare for his impending execution, Mexía replied that had the tables been turned, he would have had Santa Anna killed on the spot.

In January 1840 federalist leaders assembled at Guerrero to solidify their efforts. Meeting in convention, the insurgents announced the formation of the Republic of the Rio Grande. The proposed new nation was to be quite extensive, encompassing the Mexican states of Tamaulipas, Coahuila, Nuevo Léon, Zacatecas, Durango, Chihuahua, and New Mexico. The new president was Jesús de Cárdenas. Canales was appointed commander in chief of the republic's military forces. Carbajal was selected as secretary of the governing body known as the General Council.

The new republic was short-lived. In March 1840, Canales again met Arista on the battlefield, this time at Morales, Coahuila. The centralists handed the federalists a crushing defeat. One casualty of the battle was Antonio Zapata, the most able of the federalist military commanders. Captured, he was executed and his severed head displayed on a pole outside his home at Guerrero as a warning to other rebels. With his remaining troops, Canales fled to Texas, where he once again appealed to sympathetic Texans for help. Leading a combined Mexican-Texan column, he marched deep into Mexico, passing through Victoria and San Luis Potosi on a circuitous march that led to Saltillo. Arriving on October 25, 1840, the column found a centralist army under the command of Rafael Vásquez drawn up for battle. As the fighting began, a major contingent of Canales's Mexican supporters defected, riding across the space separating the opposing lines in order to join forces with Vásquez. In the fierce fight that followed, the Texans held out until nightfall, when they were able to slip away and make their way toward Texas. Canales, who once again evaded capture, found that support for his cause had evaporated. In November, he met with Arista at Camargo and negotiated his surrender. Like Urrea, Canales was pardoned by his government and given a commission in the centralist army.

For Mexico, the years immediately after the Texas Revolution were desperate times. Attacked from within and without, the government was unable to carry out its promised reconquest of Texas. The French threat had been thwarted and had made it possible for Santa Anna to return to power. Mexicans finally decided to put their political differences aside, at least temporarily. The cause of this truce was a growing aggressive stance on the part of the Texans. By 1840, Mexicans were ready to make a united stand against Los Diablos Tejanos (the Texan devils).

Sam Houston was no stranger to public service when he took office as president of the Republic of Texas; moreover, he was no stranger to his fellow countrymen. Born in Virginia in 1793 but reared in Tennessee, Houston had begun his professional career as a junior officer in the U.S. Army during the War of 1812. His fearlessness against the Creek Indians at the Battle of Horseshoe Bend (in present-day Alabama) caught the eye of his commander, General Andrew Jackson. Severely wounded, Houston returned home to convalesce before returning to duty. In 1818 he resigned his commission, moved to Nashville, studied law, and entered politics. Within a short time, he had joined the Masons and received an appointment as major general in the state militia. Personable and talented, Houston nevertheless owed his success in part to the backing of Andrew Jackson, who acted as mentor for the young hero of Horseshoe Bend. From 1824 to 1827, Houston served two terms in the U.S. House of Representatives. In 1827, Tennesseeans elected the 34-year-old Houston their governor. There seemed no stopping his star from rising.

Then disaster struck. Although the cause of his downfall is still shrouded in mystery, the effect was undeniable. In January 1829, Houston married Eliza Allen of Gallatin, Tennessee, a 19-year-old socialite seventeen years his junior. The marriage ended after only two months when Houston returned his bride to her father. Inexplicably, Houston then resigned as governor and moved to Indian Territory. As an adolescent, Houston once had lived among the

Cherokee of east Tennessee, earning the name "The Raven" and adoption into the tribe. Once more among his childhood friends, he found solace in drink, reportedly causing the Cherokee to rechristen him "Big Drunk." His supporters in Washington awarded Houston the position of Indian agent in charge of overseeing contracts to feed the Cherokee. Uncovering graft and corruption in the system of dispensing annuities, he traveled to Washington in 1832 to represent his Indian clients personally. Friends were appalled by his appearance, which by their accounts then more resembled a warrior from the Far West than the smooth politician they had come to know.

More trouble lay in store for Jackson's fallen protégé. Representative William Stanberry had accused Houston of profiteering in supplying the Cherokee under his care. One evening while on the streets of the nation's capital, Houston encountered the Ohio congressman and beat him with his cane in retaliation for the spurious allegations. Arrested for the attack on Stanberry, Houston was ordered to appear before the House of Representatives for trial because the crime had been committed by one U.S. congressman—alluding to Houston's former status—against another U.S. congressman.

The case proved to be the key to Houston's political comeback. Friends loaned him money for clothing, and Francis Scott Key, a prominent Washington attorney as well as author of *The Star Spangled Banner*, agreed to aid in his defense. Given the opportunity to take to the floor of the House, Houston exhibited all the wit and charm that had so impressed admirers in the past. Found guilty, he was issued a reprimand and assessed a $500 fine. Houston, having seized the opportunity to regain his popularity and public stature, chose Texas as the place to rebuild his life.

Arriving in Nacogdoches in December 1832 he began practicing law and quickly became enmeshed in local politics. Houston, having already established a national reputation, rose to a position of power and prominence in Texas that culminated in his election as president of the new republic just four years later. An experienced public servant as well as a bona fide hero of the Battles of Horseshoe Bend and San Jacinto, Houston seemed more than ready for the task ahead. In many people's minds, Houston and the Republic of Texas were one and the same.

The challenges that Houston, and those who would follow him, faced remained fairly constant. Texas needed international recognition of its independent status if it truly was to survive as an autonomous state. Additionally, the republic had to be placed on sound financial footing. Of immediate concern, however, was the need for security from both internal and external enemies. These three issues dogged the Republic of Texas from its formation in 1836 until its annexation by the United States nearly ten years later.

Houston adopted a conservative position aimed at preserving the fragile status quo, reflecting his Jacksonian Democratic view of limited government. His administration lacked funds with which to carry out any grandiose plans, let alone pay for such basic needs as defense. To the pragmatic Houston, peace was preferable to war because it was both less expensive and less disruptive to the process of nation building. One of his first acts as president was to furlough the army, essentially disbanding it. He endeavored to make peace with both Texas's internal and external enemies. He planned to use treaties to ensure that tribes such as the Cherokee remained friendly. As he explained in his inaugural address, "Treaties of peace and amity, and the maintenance of good faith with the Indians, present themselves to my mind as the most rational grounds on which to obtain their friendship."[2] With Mexico, he strove to avoid any new conflict by using the area between the Nueces River and Rio Grande as a buffer zone to limit contact, stressing that "vigilance will apprise us of their approach." Mexico's troubles greatly worked in Houston's favor, keeping that country occupied and its troops out of Texas.[3]

However, Texas could not remain under Houston's leadership for long. According to the Texas Constitution of 1836, the republic's first presidential term was to last only two years. Although all subsequent terms would run three years, no chief executive could hold office for consecutive terms. Thus, in 1838, Texas conducted a presidential campaign to find Houston's successor. The candidates included Mirabeau B. Lamar, James Collinsworth, and Peter W. Grayson. The unexpected suicides of his rivals left the field open for Lamar. Voters picked David G. Burnet, former ad interim president of the republic, as vice president.

Next to Houston, Lamar stands out as the most influential personality during the short tenure of the Republic of Texas. Born in Georgia in 1798, Lamar came to fit the image of a cultured Southern gentleman and, in many ways, epitomized the Republic of Texas

better than any of his contemporaries, including his rival, Sam
Houston. Highly intelligent and well educated, he developed an interest in literature and established a minor reputation as a poet. As
a young man in Georgia, he turned to newspaper editing as a livelihood, a path that often led to politics during this period in history. In 1823, Lamar accepted the position as secretary to Governor
George M. Troup and thereafter became linked to his employer's political faction—the Calhoun Democrats. He later moved to Columbus, where he founded a paper in support of Troup. Entering politics on his own, Lamar ran for state senator in 1828 and won.

As with Houston and his failed marriage, personal tragedy also
altered Lamar's political fortunes. Lamar's young wife, Tabitha Jordan, suffered from tuberculosis. Much of his time and attention was
focused on caring for her, prompting Lamar to resign his secretary-
ship to the governor and later to abandon his bid for reelection to the
state senate. Tabitha's death in 1830 left him shaken. With the help of
a fellow state's rights adherent, Lamar revived the *Columbus En-
quirer*, which served as a vehicle for his strident anti-Jackson views.
An avid supporter of the doctrine of nullification, his attacks on
Old Hickory sound much like the ones he later unleashed on Mexico, its leaders, and Houston. Attempts to return to public office
proved unsuccessful. In 1835 he traveled to Texas where he met such
other Georgians as James W. Fannin and was impressed with the opportunities the region offered. He returned to Georgia to make
preparations for relocating to his new home.

The revolt against the centralist government erupted in Lamar's
absence. By April 1836, however, Lamar was back in Texas and serving as a private in the army commanded by Houston. During a skirmish with Santa Anna's troops on the afternoon of April 20, Lamar
won the admiration and respect of his comrades when he risked his
life to save several Texans in danger of being run down by Mexican
lancers. The next day, just hours before the start of the Battle of San
Jacinto, Lamar was appointed colonel in recognition of his valor and
placed in command of Houston's cavalry. In the weeks and months
that followed, Lamar occupied several high-profile positions, first as
secretary of war in Burnet's cabinet and then as major general in the
Texas Army. Lamar resigned his commission when the soldiers in
the field refused to accept him as their commander. Their action was
not a rejection of him personally but rather a display of contempt by
the volunteers toward Burnet's policies. Lamar retired to civilian life

but not out of the spotlight. The same voters who chose Houston as president in 1836 elected Lamar vice president of the republic.

Houston and Lamar developed an intense dislike for one another that turned into a caustic political rivalry. A schism developed that separated Texans into two factions: Houstonites and Lamarites. It was not unexpected then that Lamar's inauguration in December 1838 ushered in a reversal of Houston's policies. While Houston had been intent on safeguarding the infant republic, Lamar had visions of building a continental empire.

For Lamar, Texas's future lay in following its own path. He warned his countrymen about the consequences of joining the United States: "I cannot regard the annexation of Texas to the American Union in any other light than as the grave of all her hopes of happiness and greatness; and if, contrary to the present aspect of affairs, the amalgamation shall hereafter take place, I shall feel that the blood of our ma[r]tyred heroes had been shed in vain."[4] Thus, Lamar viewed the sacrifice of men such as James Bowie, David Crockett, William B. Travis, and a whole host of lesser-known heroes as the down payment on Texas's prosperity.

Lamar soon announced the course of action he would pursue while president. In his inaugural address he proclaimed a new attitude toward Texas's foes. "Preferring peace, but not adverse to war, I shall be ever ready to adjust all differences with our enemies by friendly discussion and arrangement, at the same time be equally prompt to adopt either offensive or defensive operations, as their disposition and our own safety may render necessary."[5] Shortly afterward, Lamar told the Texas Congress, "My great solicitude on the subject of frontier protection has partially overruled the repugnance I have always felt for standing armies."[6] Overcoming the American prejudice against the regular military, Lamar stated that a "permanent and efficient force" was needed due to the "present disturbed condition of our foreign and Indian relations." He called for expanded trade to place the republic on a sound financial footing, aided by the establishment of a national bank. Revealing his literary roots, Lamar proclaimed the need to establish a system of education, telling the Texas Congress that the "cultivated mind is the guardian genius of democracy."[7] Revealing his vision of empire, he announced that it was time to end talk of annexation to the United States because Texas had its own destiny to fulfill.[8]

The "disturbed condition of Indian relations" attracted Lamar's attention as he assumed his office. In particular, he decided that the Cherokee issue must be settled. This tribe, which had relatives in the United States and Indian Territory, had drifted into Texas around 1807. Spanish officials welcomed them for the same reasons that they later welcomed Moses Austin and other settlers: Settlers were needed, and the Cherokee had won the appellation as one of the "five civilized tribes" of North America owing to their acceptance of many of the cultural traits of Americans. While the acculturation helped to make many individual Cherokee who owned farms and even plantations materially successful, prevailing prejudices against Indians in general prevented the Cherokee from gaining acceptance from the majority of nineteenth-century Americans. The Georgian Lamar shared the view prevalent in his home state, which had supported Andrew Jackson's Indian policy and its outcome, the Trail of Tears. The Cherokee, in his view, did not have a legitimate claim to the land they occupied in Texas. Furthermore, he warned that despite repeated acts of clemency and kindness shown to all Indians, "The [settler's] wife and infant afford as rich a trophy to the *scalping knife,* as the warrior who falls in the vigor of manhood and pride of chivalry."[9] The story of Lamar's campaign to expel the Cherokee from Texas is part of the overall story of Indian policy in Jacksonian America.

The Texas Cherokee had become familiar with the practice of gaining a title for one's land and had applied to Spanish officials for a grant. None was issued before Mexico became an independent republic. Mexican officials, too, failed to satisfy the Cherokee claim prior to the eruption of the revolt in Texas. The Cherokee, led by Duwali (called Chief Bowl by the Texans), were caught in the middle. Siding with the Texans would jeopardize their standing as loyal Mexicans, thereby endangering the claim to land. But siding against the Texans meant that they would earn the animosity of their American neighbors who would surely look to settle the score should the revolt succeed. Chief Bowl indicated his intention to remain neutral, but the delegates gathered for the Consultation wanted assurance that the Cherokee would not enter the war on the side of the centralists. A treaty to placate the tribe seemed to be in order.

In 1835 the officers of the provisional government had named commissioners to negotiate with Chief Bowl. One of these officials was Sam Houston, who seemed a logical choice due to his high rank as commander of the yet-to-exist regular army. Moreover, he was an adopted member of the tribe and someone who might be expected to have influence over it. On January 28, 1836, with military affairs in disarray owing to the dispute between Governor Henry Smith and the General Council, the governor furloughed Houston, which freed him to negotiate a treaty with the Cherokee. On February 23, 1836 (the same day that Santa Anna entered San Antonio and began the siege of the Alamo), Houston signed a treaty with Chief Bowl guaranteeing the Cherokee title to land in east Texas in return for maintaining friendly relations with the new Texas government. Following the revolution, the treaty languished in the Texas senate despite Houston's efforts to have it ratified. In December 1837 the Texas senate declared the treaty void, leaving the Cherokee with no legal claim to the land they occupied.

The Cherokee's situation was about to become even worse, due in part to machinations from Mexico. Texans' fears about an Indian uprising were valid, because Mexican officials hoped to enlist the Cherokee and other tribes in the fight to regain Texas. Efforts to fan Indian resentment during the revolution had largely been unsuccessful, but the plan had support among Mexicans and some Mexican-Texans. In August 1838, Tejano residents at Nacogdoches, led by Vicente Córdova, rose up in arms. The town had been a major population center prior to the formation of the Republic of Texas, and Tejano residents resented the influx of Americans and the subsequent loss of political power and social position they had experienced. Declaring that they would not tolerate the situation any longer, Córdova and his supporters proposed an alliance with local tribes in a war against the Republic of Texas. The Córdova Rebellion, as the affair was called, was short-lived, being extinguished before the month was out, but its ramifications were far-reaching.

Chief Bowl denied involvement in the plot, but evidence surfaced implicating the Cherokee and other tribes. In August, documents were found on the body of a Mexican killed near the Red River that detailed the Mexican government's plan to incite the Texas Indians into warring against the Texans. A diary entry showed that Julián Pedro Miracle, the dead agent, had visited Chief Bowl while on his trip through Texas and had supposedly extracted a promise of cooperation. In May 1839 more evidence came to light when another Mexican agent, Manuel Flores, was killed near the North San Gabriel River. More documents were found that outlined the impending Mexican-sanctioned Indian uprising. Chief Bowl, supported by his friend Houston, continued to deny the charges, but time had run out for the Cherokee.

Lamar and his cabinet decided that the Cherokee must leave Texas and cross the Red River into U.S.-owned Indian Territory. In July 1839, Lamar sent commissioners to Chief Bowl's village to arrange for the Cherokee's immediate removal. Although they reluctantly agreed to abandon their homes in exchange for a monetary settlement to offset their losses, the chief and others balked at the stipulation calling for the Texas military officials to oversee their expulsion. The commissioners declared them hostile, setting the stage for a brief but decisive military campaign called the Cherokee War. Troops accompanying the commissioners, commanded by Thomas Jefferson Rusk and Edward Burleson, marched on the Cherokee village. The two days of fighting that followed left Chief Bowl dead and the Cherokee routed. From the Texan point of view, the Battle of the Neches settled the Cherokee issue as the remnants of the tribe made their way to either Indian Territory or Mexico.

Another tribe, the Comanche, proved more difficult and deadlier for the Texans. The 1836 attack on Fort Parker was only one in a continuing series of raids by this fiercely independent and warlike people. Unlike the Cherokee and other tribes that inhabited east Texas and who farmed and lived in their own settlements, the Comanche were nomads whose range extended from the Red River deep into northern Mexico. Their lifestyle had been revolutionized by the acquisition of the horse and gun. They had mastered the art of hit-and-run tactics, sweeping across Texas and striking terror into Mexicans and Texans alike. Often traveling by night under the light of a full moon, the Comanche struck isolated homesteads and ranches on the outskirts of such towns as San Antonio, carrying off livestock and captives.

Texas officials tried both diplomacy and force to deal with this serious problem. Companies of rangers were formed to patrol the routes most often used by the Comanche on their raids. When raids occurred, the rangers pursued the culprits, who were laden with booty, sometimes catching and engaging them in battle. Rangers also sought out and attacked Indian camps, not discriminating among men, women, and children during these brief but heated skirmishes. The cycle of raid and retaliation began to wear on both sides, creating a desire for an end to the constant hostility and fear it generated.

In 1840 the Comanche signaled that they would be willing to make peace with the Texans and sent messengers to San Antonio to arrange for a meeting with officials there. The Texans agreed to meet with the Comanche under the following conditions: They must (1) cease their raids, (2) return property taken in previous raids, and (3) free all captives. The meeting was set for March 19, 1840, to be held at the courthouse (also called the Council House) on the civil plaza in San Antonio. That morning sixty-five Comanche men, women, and children rode into town. Instead of bringing in all the captives as had been expected, the Comanche had brought in only Matilda Lockwood, a young girl who had been captured several months earlier. Angry that the Comanche had not followed instructions, the Texans grew even more upset when they saw that Lockwood had been disfigured, her nose having been burned away by repeated branding with a hot coal. Inside the Council House, the situation grew tense when officials told the chiefs who had come into town that they would not be allowed to leave until all prisoners were released. A fierce fight broke out between the Comanche and Texans that spilled out into the plaza and the adjacent town lots. During the Council House Fight, as the affair was called, soldiers and townspeople pursued the Comanche who tried to flee the town. In the end, thirty-five Comanche were killed, and twenty-seven were retained as hostages. Seven soldiers and civilians died, and eight more were wounded. A lone Comanche woman was released to tell her people what had happened and that they must bring in the rest of the white captives.

The disastrous meeting hardened relations between the Texans and Comanche. A few more captives were freed, but others remained in the hands of the Comanche, although one of the survivors reported that several Texan captives were tortured and murdered in retaliation for the death of the chiefs. The Comanche hostages, who reportedly were treated well and lightly guarded, slipped away one by one. Rangers patrolled the frontier and small raids continued. Then, in August 1840, the largest Comanche raid of the republic era swept across Texas. In the first week of that month, small parties of

Comanche and their Kiowa allies slipped out of their traditional homeland in the Hill Country west of present-day Austin. Once assembled, the war party numbered somewhere between 400 and 600 warriors. On the afternoon of August 6 the citizens of Victoria were startled to find their town surrounded and under attack. Retreating to their homes, the townspeople managed to keep the attackers at bay. The presence of large herds of horses in the vicinity worked to their advantage, because the Indians' attention was diverted by this valuable prize. An estimated 1,500 horses and mules were taken by the Comanche when they broke off the engagement. The following morning the Comanche returned once more to Victoria but soon left when resistance appeared. Abandoning their normal practice of hit and run, the Comanche did not ride for home but instead expanded the raid.

The war party next attacked the village of Linnville on the Gulf Coast. A point of entry into Texas, Linnville had become a commercial center and as such contained not only homes but warehouses. Even so, it was really only a collection of scattered buildings. The residents, who realized their peril, rushed to the beach, where they boarded several merchant ships anchored offshore. From their shipboard safety, they watched Linnville be looted and burned. Loaded with colorful bolts of cloth and wearing top hats and carrying umbrellas, the raiders left toward evening, this time headed back to Comanchería. At least twenty-one townspeople and ranchers had fallen victim to the Comanche during the raid. Several more were beginning a period of Comanche captivity.

Word of the Great Comanche Raid spread. Small bands of rangers and armed citizens trailed the raiders as they made their way back to the Hill Country. Frequently changing to fresh horses from the large herd they had captured, the Comanche stayed ahead of their pursuers. Unable to catch the raiders, the Texans prepared to intercept them on the plains before they could reach the Edwards Plateau and escape into the hills beyond.

The raid, begun in retaliation for the death of twelve chiefs at the Council House Fight, led to the Battle of Plum Creek. This was the type of fight that gave the Texans the advantage. The Comanche, who usually avoided pitched battles where the two sides were massed together, were forced to fight or abandon their plunder. On the morning of August 12 a large force of militia, rangers, and armed citizens led by Felix Huston and Edward Burleson encountered the retreating Comanche on Plum Creek near present-day San Marcos. More than eighty Comanche died in the ensuing battle and pursuit that followed. Texans losses were fewer than ten. Much of the looted property was recovered and the owners allowed to claim what was theirs.

The Comanche, while still remaining a formidable foe, suffered a serious setback with their defeat at Plum Creek. Compounding their trouble, in October a Texan expedition traveled 300 miles inside Comanchería and destroyed a major encampment. The defeat in August and destruction of the village two months later put an end to some of the bolder attacks on Texan settlements. By October 1844 renewed negotiations resulted in the Treaty of Tehuacana Creek, in which the Texans and Comanche vowed "that they will forever live in peace, and always meet as friends and brothers." [10] The peace held for some time, but the Comanche eventually resumed their time-tested hit-and-run tactics and continued to raid the frontier for more than thirty years. After Texas's annexation in 1845 the problem of controlling the Comanche and other hostile tribes became the duty of the U.S. Army.

Lamar's efforts to develop the frontier involved picking a new site for the capital of the republic. The Constitutional Convention originally met in March 1836 at Washington-on-the-Brazos. The advance of Santa Anna's forces had caused the government to flee to Harrisburg and Galveston. After the revolution the towns of Velasco and Columbia hosted the government before Houston ordered the capital moved to the new town named in his honor. Beginning in December 1838 the town of Houston served as the center of government for Texas. Crowded and dirty, as were so many settlements spawned by speculation, Houston had plenty of saloons but lacked housing and office space. However, it constantly buzzed with activity. A bill to move the capital to La Grange passed the Texas Congress but was vetoed by President Houston. The question of a suitable place for the government to officiate surfaced again after the election of Lamar.

Lamar believed that moving the capital west would stimulate settlement of the frontier. Not only would elected officials and their staffs be drawn there, but so would businessmen who hoped to build the new town and supply its residents with all their needs from lodging to printing. Once established, the capital would grow as more people chose to make it their home. Within a short time the capital would become a bastion of civilization in what was previously a wilderness. A committee sent to survey prospective sites returned with a recommendation to relocate the seat of government to the east bank of the Colorado River north of the Old San Antonio Road on the edge of the Texas Hill Country. Besides abundant water, the site had wood for building and rich loam that could sustain agriculture. In January 1839 the relocation plan was approved, although governmental officials did not arrive until the following October. First called Waterloo, the town was renamed Austin in honor of the famous *empresario* who had died shortly after the Texas Revolution. Sam Houston's political enemies, Lamar among them, were glad to have struck a blow at their adversary by wresting the seat of government out of Houston's home territory.

Moving the capital also revealed among Texans a division along regional lines. The inhabitants in the area of the old *empresario* grants and the residents of the newly established communities such as Houston and Galveston favored concentrating the republic's efforts on developing these more commercially viable parts of the nation. Success there would show the world that Texas had lived up to its promises and expectations. Conversely, Texans who had moved to the frontier regions wanted their government's support in such matters as road building, postal routes, and especially defense. The east-west split was reflected in the policies and action of Houston's and Lamar's respective administrations.

Unlike the conservative Houston, Lamar wanted not only to settle the frontier but to extend the limits of the republic. On December 19, 1836, the Texas Congress had passed legislation defining the boundary of Texas to include the following area: "beginning at the mouth of the Sabine river, and running west along the Gulf of Mexico three leagues from land, to the mouth of the Rio Grande, thence up the principle stream of said river to its source, thence due north to the forty-second degree of north latitude, thence along the boundary line as defined in the treaty between the Unites States and Spain." [11]

According to Texas officials, New Mexico belonged to the Republic of Texas. Lamar sought to accomplish two objectives by sending an expedition to Santa Fe. First, Texas could cash in on the lucrative trade that flowed northeastward into Missouri. Why not divert Mexican silver to Texas, where it would help stabilize the republic's disastrous financial condition? Second, such an expedition would bolster Texas's claim to New Mexico. News that the New Mexicans had revolted against the centralists in 1837 fueled rumors that the region's inhabitants were unhappy with the Mexican government and were ready to establish ties with the Texans. Unable to obtain congressional approval for the plan, Lamar launched the venture on his own authority.

The Santa Fe Expedition was a massive undertaking not unlike those made by earlier Spanish and French explorers into uncharted territory. Lamar appointed 26-year-old Hugh McLeod, who had immigrated from Georgia at the end of the Texas Revolution, to command the battalion of volunteers sent to escort twenty-one wagons filled with merchandise. The column numbered 321 soldiers, teamsters, and traders. Officially designated the Santa Fe Pioneers, the force was thought to be more than adequate to handle any situation that might arise either on the journey or once their destination was reached. But problems quickly appeared that should have warned that the expedition was in trouble even before it began. The column made a late start from Austin, not leaving until mid-June 1841, when water and grass were already in short supply. McLeod became ill and had to remain behind while the caravan continued without him. Once reunited with his command, he was unable to reestablish control over the independent-minded volunteers. His quartermaster decided that the beef herd accompanying the column was too small to feed the expedition, so more time was lost rounding up additional cattle. No one in the expedition knew the route from Texas to Santa Fe, causing the Texans to strike off to New Mexico with only a vague idea of how to get there.

Cautious men predicted disaster for the expedition. Emerging in late July from a heavily thicketed region known as the Cross Timbers, the expedition mistook the Wichita River for the Red River, which they had planned to followed to its intersection with the Santa Fe Trail out of Missouri. More time passed while the lost travelers tried to determine where the expedition was. Shortly afterward, signs of Comanche and Kiowa appeared, signifying that their hunting ranges had been reached. Several stragglers even fell victim to these old enemies who shadowed the Texans. Finally reaching the

Llano Estacado, the expedition realized that the escarpment was too steep for the wagons to ascend. With both summer and supplies running out, McLeod decided to send an advance party ahead to New Mexico to obtain a guide and fresh provisions while he, the wagons, and the rest of the troops remained behind. The advance party entered New Mexico only to learn that rumors of the friendly welcome awaiting them were untrue and that the New Mexicans were prepared to resist what the governor, Manuel Armijo, had characterized as an invasion. The outnumbered advance party surrendered to New Mexican authorities on September 12, 1841. Five days later McLeod surrendered the remainder of the expedition near modern-day Tucumcari, New Mexico. Instead of liberators the Santa Fe Pioneers found themselves prisoners.

Disarmed and their horses seized, the Texans were marched on foot from New Mexico to Mexico City more than 1,000 miles away. Closely watched and forced to match the pace of their guards, anyone who lagged behind was killed. The prisoners who survived the march were put to work repairing roads around the Mexican capital. Some of those forced to labor were quartered in an old mill called Molino del Rey within sight of the hilltop fortress of Chapultepec. Others later were transferred to an old stone fort, Castle San Carlos (better known as Perote Prison), outside Jalapa where they, too, performed forced labor. These locations became part of the lore of the conflict and would conjure up images of horror whenever mentioned.

In his zeal to expand the Republic of Texas, Lamar handed Mexico a victory for which that country did not have to fire a single shot. Blasted by the Texas Congress for launching the disastrous expedition without their consent, he ended his term as president under a hail of criticism. His successor, who took office in December 1842, was none other than Sam Houston. "Old San Jacinto," whose policy had been to avoid provoking Mexico into renewed hostilities, must have felt a modicum of satisfaction as well as vindication as he once again became the chief executive of the republic. The storm he had warned against was about to break.

∽ The centralist faction in Mexico had remained in power despite the threats posed to it by the federalist disturbances and the Pastry War. The latter event had even propelled Santa Anna back into the limelight and, for a short period from March 1839 until the following July, he again held the office of president of Mexico. In October 1841 the Mexican Congress cloaked Santa Anna with dictatorial powers in the aftermath of the Santa Fe Expedition. With much of their internal and external problems settled for the time being, the Mexican government led by Santa Anna decided that the time had come to remind Texans that Mexico had not abandoned the idea of reclaiming its wayward territory.

Orders to renew hostilities with Texas reached General Mariano Arista at his Monterrey headquarters in early December 1841. As military commander of northern Mexico, Arista was instructed to prepare a small mobile force for a swift and unexpected raid into Texas. The mission, according to Santa Anna, would demonstrate that Mexico was not too weak and divided to respond when attacked. He wrote, "Inaction is not only perilous, but even dishonorable for the Nation." The main focus of the raid was San Antonio, where the soldiers were to "surprise its garrison and take it captive, or to put it to the knife should it offered obstinate resistance." A smaller party was to strike in the Goliad area as a diversion, to create confusion among the Texans. In addition to restoring Mexico's tarnished military reputation, the raid would forestall any more incursions into Mexican territory such as that attempted by the Santa Fe Pioneers.[12]

Although the raid did not go exactly as planned, it returned Mexican troops to Texas soil. Colonel Rafael Vásquez, who had faced the Texans near Saltillo during the Federalist War in 1840, commanded the San Antonio wing of the operation, which left the Rio Grande on February 24, 1842, with 400 men. Word of their advance proceeded them, however, allowing Texans from the towns of Gonzalez and Seguín to reinforce San Antonio. Instructed by Arista to avoid assaulting any fortified position, Vásquez parleyed with the Texans, who numbered about 260 and were prepared to defend the town. Bloodshed was prevented when the Texans agreed to withdraw and allow Vásquez to enter the town unopposed. Proclaimed the colonel to his government, "The National flag is once again flying over the city of Béjar, and the Mexican Eagles are again treading the soil they had been deprived of for the length of six years."[13] Mexican troops occupied the town from March 5 through March 8.

The eastern wing of the raid, numbering only about 150, did not fare as well. Its commander, Captain Ramón Valera, found that his men's horses were unable to hold up under the rigorous demands of his rapid movement into Texas. Attempts to send detachments ahead to strike at Goliad and Refugio failed. Nevertheless, Valera's command defeated a force of 300 Lipan Apache and Tancahue Indians it encountered on the Santa Gertrudis River. By mid-March, both Vásquez and Valera had withdrawn, leaving Texas once more to the Texans.

One effect of Vásquez's raid on San Antonio was to drive a wedge between Juan N. Seguín and the Republic of Texas. Vásquez approached several of the town's residents with implications that Seguín, who was then serving as mayor, had assisted him in his advance into Texas. Although many of the old Texan supporters discounted the story as an attempt by the Mexican officer to discredit him, other more recent immigrants made it dangerous for Seguín to remain in Texas. Fearing for his family's safety, he relocated to northern Mexico.

Despite the consternation it had caused, the raid fell short of Santa Anna's expectations. He castigated Arista for Vásquez's failure either to capture or kill the garrison at San Antonio. The chagrined army commander reminded the president that the colonel had been directed to refrain from engaging fortified positions and that the Texans had occupied the town and were prepared to defend it if attacked. Arista justified Vásquez's withdrawal from San Antonio after having captured it, writing his chief that "I can assure Y.E. [Your Excellency], that he would have known how to hold the outpost he is now occupying, had the instructions been to this effect."[14] Arista received a reply from José Maria Tornel, once again serving as secretary of war and navy to Santa Anna, who demanded that Vásquez be sent to the capital to explain his conduct:

> His Excellency the Provisional President has taken cognizance, with utmost disgust, of everything the said General has related, since he has failed in his principle duties, as the government did not send him to occupy Béjar, but to take by surprise and capture or put to the knife the garrison of adventurers who had taken possession of that town, as well as of Goliad and Cópano, a stroke that would have brought great honor to the army by again opening that campaign in which the Mexican troops would present themselves on the offensive.[15]

One concern expressed by Tornel was the impression that their enemies might form that "500 Mexican dragoons did not dare to match their arms with 260 Texan footmen, poorly disciplined and worse situated."[16] He scolded, "The recent conduct of the gallant General Armijo [in capturing the Santa Fe Pioneers] should have served as a model for General Vásquez who had ample opportunity to imitate him."[17] The adventurers who occupied Texas "must be made to surrender or be exterminated" whenever they were encountered.[18] Captain Valera also came in for criticism for his actions in the area around Goliad. Tornel insisted that the Texans could not be allowed to think that the Mexicans had left because they were afraid to meet them on the battlefield. Additionally, the affair had alerted the Texans to Mexico's intention and, as in the case of the revolt of 1835–36, reinforcements from the United States could now be expected to rush to their countrymen's aid. Moreover, loyal Mexicans who had been delighted to see that their country had not forgotten them had been left once again at the mercy of the Texans. Only another expedition could wipe out the perceived failure of the first and provide aid and comfort to Texas's Mexican citizenry. Santa Anna assigned this important mission to a trusted lieutenant, General Adrián Woll, an officer who had served him as quartermaster general of the Mexican Army during the Texas Campaign. Seized and held prisoner by the Texans in the days following San Jacinto, although protected by a flag of truce, Woll took delight in his mission to punish his old foes.

A clash of arms occurred even before Woll gathered his force for the new campaign. As Santa Anna had warned, the raid had drawn help from the United States. Recruiters from Texas actively sought "emigrants," a euphemism for volunteers with promises of land and plunder. In June 1842, Colonel Antonio Canales learned at his post on the Rio Grande that a force of volunteers was assembling in the vicinity of Corpus Christi near the mouth of the Nueces River for the purpose of marching on Matamoros and other towns along the river. He gathered his troops to strike before the descent could be made. On July 7, Canales attacked the Texans camped near the old site of Lipantitlán and drove them from their hilltop position. The Mexicans killed twenty-two of the volunteers while losing only four men. The spoils included a large quantity of small arms and three flags, including the banner of the Galveston Invincibles.[19] In typical military fashion, both sides claimed victory, but the fact remained that Canales had blunted the push to Matamoros.

Despite Santa Anna's wish that troops be sent back to Texas immediately, the second expedition took several months to organize. By September 1, 1842, however, General Woll's column consisting of 1,082 troops of all military branches (cavalry, infantry, and artillery) was marching northward toward San Antonio. Woll's orders were for him not only to capture the town but to fight them, beat them, and take prisoner any armed Texans he encountered. Once having secured San Antonio, a side expedition was to be launched against Goliad. His government instructed Woll that he must occupy Texas soil for at least one month so that the world would see that this was not just a brief incursion but a full-scale military campaign. The Texans must be brought to battle to dispel the notion that the Mexicans feared them. Woll knew that this was not to be just a repeat of Vásquez's earlier raid.[20]

The expedition arrived at San Antonio early on the morning of September 10, 1842. Woll had avoided detection by the Texans on his march by taking a less frequently used route than the one traveled by Vásquez. He had a guide who knew the area well: Juan N. Seguín, who had removed his family from Texas, had been ordered to assist Woll as part of the agreement that allowed the former rebel to stay in Mexico. Several townspeople discovered Woll's approach and rode out to request that he not enter San Antonio, saying that the Texans would put up a fight and make them join in. Woll took them into custody and used the cover of darkness to place his troops around the town in order to prevent unauthorized entrance or exit. Moving quickly before the sun rose, his troops seized the main plaza before the Texans had time to react. Mexican soldiers occupied many of the buildings on the perimeter of the plaza and unlimbered two artillery pieces, readying them for immediate use. The Texans, who Woll estimated to number approximately 150, had gathered at the home of Samuel A. Maverick on the northwest corner of the plaza. The house was next to the Veramendi House, the property that once had belonged to James Bowie's in-laws. Maverick himself had been a member of the Alamo garrison and had escaped death when he was sent to Washington-on-the-Brazos to represent his comrades at the Constitutional Convention. The Mexican troops opened fire on the house, the Texans returned fire. After about thirty minutes a white flag appeared, and the Texans requested a cease-fire so the following offer could be made to Woll: The Texans would lay down their arms if the general would allow them to leave town un-molested. During the parley, many of the Texans slipped away, apparently escaping by way of the river that ran behind Maverick's home. When the offer was refused the fifty-two Texans who remained behind surrendered unconditionally. Woll reported that the fight, although brief, had been fierce, with Texan casualties numbering twelve killed and three wounded while the Mexican losses numbered one killed and eighteen wounded. Texan accounts place their own casualties much lower.

The Mexicans had a military victory complete with prisoners. And what prisoners these were! Many area residents had come to San Antonio to attend a session of district court. Thus, Woll's captives included lawyers, judges, and other officials as well as prominent men who had come either to watch or to participate in the trials. One of the captives was James W. Robinson, former lieutenant governor of the provisional government of 1835–36. The prospect of even greater successes lay ahead as Woll dispatched part of his command to carry out the second objective of his mission, a foray in the direction of Goliad from San Antonio.

Woll remained in San Antonio while his detachment rode off to the east. On September 16 the general had the pleasure of celebrating the thirty-second anniversary of Father Hidalgo's pronouncement, which had started the independence movement in 1810. He prepared to leave on September 18, having learned that a large number of Texans were organizing to recapture San Antonio from his soldiers. That morning, however, scouts reported that the Texans were approaching San Antonio, prompting Woll to attack. The clash took place on Salado Creek, eight miles east of town. Even though instructed by his government not to engage the enemy if they occupied a wooded position, Woll counted on his superior numbers to carry the day. The results were such that both the Mexicans and Texans could claim victory. The numbers of casualties given by the opposing sides do not agree, as both claimed to have killed more than 100 of the enemy while their own losses were minimal. Woll's men definitely mauled a party of fifty-three Texans commanded by Nicholas Mosby Dawson as they attempted to join the rest of their countrymen. Surrounded and pounded by artillery, only two managed to escape while thirty-six Texans were killed and fifteen were taken prisoner. The Battle of Salado Creek and Dawson's Massacre added another bitter chapter to the ongoing struggle between Mexico and Texas.

Texans were outraged. Not only had the raids by Vásquez, Valera, Canales, and Woll shown that the Mexico still posed a serious threat to the republic's security, but national honor was also at stake. Could enemy troops be allowed to cross into Texas and carry off its citizens into captivity? Mexico must be punished, the prisoners freed, and honor restored. Calls for action swept across Texas.

The Republic of Texas had a well-established martial tradition, but by no means was it ready for a war with Mexico. The Texas military establishment mirrored that of the United States and drew on the same long-standing traditions that defined the military establishment of that day. Evidence of the connection appeared in the early days of the Texas Revolution when the members of the provisional government, themselves immigrants from the United States, had sought to create a military force in the image of their homeland. This force was to be composed of regulars, volunteers, and militia. The Provisional Government decreed on November 26, 1835, that a regular army be organized and disciplined according to the rules that regulated the U.S. Army. That body even placed an order for 100 copies of Scott's *Infantry Drill,* twenty-six copies of Crop's *Discipline and Regulations,* and thirty-six copies of McComb's *School of the Soldier* with which to train their new army.[21] Sam Houston, named commander of this nonexistent army and charged with the duty of raising a force of regular soldiers from scratch, displayed his familiarity of military science when sending procurement agents to the United States to locate basic military necessities for his fledgling force. Writing on December 30, 1835, from Fort Jesup, Louisiana, one agent informed Houston that he was forwarding the following blank forms: "a Muster Roll, a Monthly return of a Company, [and] a Quarterly return of a return of Ordnance." Also sent were "an annual estimate of the clothing required by a Company for the following year" as well as a copy of the regulations of the U.S. Army.[22] These examples reveal how much, even at the dawn of the revolution, Texas looked to the United States as its military role model and attempted to replicate its army. Clear to anyone who studies the revolution is that creating a regular army in the midst of war had proved much more difficult to do than its designers had imagined.

The new government of the Republic of Texas stuck to the plan to imitate the national and state armies of the United States. On November 21, 1836, the Texas Congress adopted for its own force of regulars a slightly revised version of a document entitled the *Articles of War* that governed the U.S. Army.[23] They acted in a similar manner when on December 6, 1836, the Texas Congress essentially combined and adopted the May 8, 1792, and February 28, 1795, militia laws of the United States.[24] These two laws outlined such details as who would serve, how the militia was to be organized, and what punishment was appropriate for someone who evaded this important republican responsibility.[25]

The Texas Army got off to a slow start. Houston believed the republic could not afford a large standing army, and his policy of avoiding conflict made the need for such a force unnecessary. Minor incidents could be handled on an ad hoc basis by the militia or local residents. Besides, like many Jacksonians, Houston philosophically opposed a regular army on the grounds that citizen-solders, not hirelings, were the proper guardians of a republic. Thus, building an army was a low priority to Houston. Lamar's election to the presidency marked a change in Texas's military policy. On January 23, 1839, the Texas Congress moved to revitalize its regular force by ordering 1,000 copies of *Regulations for the Army of the Republic,* a book that mirrored one in use by the U.S. Army since the mid-1820s. Soon purchasing agents were placing orders for uniforms, arms, camp equipment, and everything else needed to outfit an army. Recruiting stations were established to enlist soldiers, and the Texas Congress liberally granted commissions to men who would make up its officer corps. Albert Sidney Johnston served as secretary of war, providing a guiding hand for the new army.

However, the republic's attempt proved no more successful than the earlier effort to create a dependable permanent military force. Although supplies were readily procured, finding recruits for the Texas Army was difficult, and keeping them proved even more difficult. Many of the officers commissioned by the Texas Congress quarreled with one another and with the lawmakers. Additionally, organizing the militia of the new republic was painstakingly slow and lacked the support of the citizens who were to fill its ranks. In these respects, the Texas military establishment did mimic that of the United States, unfortunately replicating its vices instead of its virtues.

On election to a second term as president, Houston had his revenge on Lamar, striking at his rival's beloved army. Dissatisfied with its performance and unable to pay for its upkeep, opponents of the Texas Army, urged on by Houston, pushed a bill through the Texas Congress on January 18, 1841, that dealt the regular service a death blow. It abolished many positions, both staff and line, and imposed a moratorium on recruiting. Denied additional funding, the Texas Army ceased to exist, strangled to death by Houston's administration.

Even before scrapping its regular army in 1841, the Texas Congress had turned to alternative means of meeting military emergencies. On December 5, 1836, Texas lawmakers created a 280-man battalion of mounted riflemen to protect the frontier. Troops of this type often were called mounted gunmen or rangers and, while not new or even unique to Texas, they were ideally suited for its frontier conditions. Texas's lawmakers also instituted a tradition popular in urban areas of the United States of granting special concessions to volunteers who agreed to organize companies for community defense. Hence sprang up Houston's Milam Guards, the Houston Artillery Company, the Fannin [County] Guards, Austin's Travis Guards, the Galveston Guards, and the Galveston Artillery Company. Units such as these were designated volunteer militia to distinguish them from the common militia. It is important to note, however, that both the rangers and volunteer militia, although appearing somewhat independent, operated under "the same rules, regulations, and restrictions of the regular army" of the republic and as such were responsible to the government.[26]

Texas had met its military emergencies mainly by relying on citizen-soldiers. In addition to the officially sanctioned ranger companies organized for frontier defense, citizens turned out and organized ad hoc units in response to Comanche raids and other crises. Reflecting the democratic principles in which they believed, the men elected one of their own to lead them. No official term of service existed, and the group disbanded once the emergency had disappeared. Dissatisfied members could hold new elections to replace old commanders who had fallen out of favor. Any member was also free to quit the expedition whenever he wished. While the system, sometimes dubbed "the frontier military tradition," worked in cases of small local alarms, it was extremely unsuited for responding to the incursions by Mexican troops. The system's main failing was the inherent confusion caused by the rejection of formal discipline. Independent companies strove to maintain their independence even when the situation called for cooperation and a unified command. In an army of equals, everyone was a potential commander with the right to express his own opinion freely.

The regular army of the republic had played an important role prior to its demise. Its troops took part in the Cherokee War, the Council House Fight, and the Battle of Plum Creek. Officially authorized to consist of one regiment of cavalry, one regiment of artillery, and four regiments of infantry, only one regiment of the latter corps was actually recruited, and even it never reached full strength. Not only had the army been legislated out of existence; much of its equipment, including arms, had been issued to the Santa Fe Pioneers and had fallen into the hands of the New Mexicans.

Citizens responded to the Mexican raids well before their government reacted. Impromptu companies rushed to San Antonio during both the Vásquez and Woll raids. Ranger captains such as John Coffee Hays led their men to San Antonio. It was a force composed of these elements that challenged Woll on Salado Creek. Units like these also shadowed the Mexicans on their retreat to the Rio Grande. The Texans, however, expected and demanded action from their president in this time of crisis.

Houston's response to the raids angered many of his constituents. The republic, he reminded them, did not have money to wage a war against Mexico. The raids, although annoying, did not herald a new invasion: Defense, not offense, he counseled, was the proper course to follow. Santa Anna was only rattling his saber, and he could not possibly mount a major campaign to reconquer Texas. Even many ardent Houston supporters rejected this idea as shameful and cowardly.

Houston continued to pursue this controversial course even though he knew that most Texans opposed him on this issue. He finally agreed to call a special session of the Texas Congress in the summer following Vásquez's raid but declared that Austin was too exposed to danger and ordered Texas's lawmakers instead to convene at Houston. Lured there by the promise of action, Houston angered them when he vetoed a war bill that would have mobilized the militia for a campaign against Mexico, financed by the sale of

10 million acres of public land. They had even thrown in a plum for Houston himself; he would command the invasion! Calling the plan unfeasible, he failed to be swayed. Although the Texas Congress passed the bill over his protest, it was an empty gesture, as a project of this magnitude needed the cooperation of all branches of government and no funds existed to pay for the mobilization.

Woll's raid only increased the demand for immediate action. Unable to remain passive any longer, Houston ordered a political ally, Alexander Somervell, to take charge of Texans who had gathered near San Antonio in preparation for an attack on Mexico. Independent as ever, the men he was to command accepted him as their general with skepticism and resentment. They would much rather be allowed to elect their own man, someone such as Vice President Edward Burleson, but Houston did not give them a choice. With this unpopular decision as a backdrop, the expedition began on a sour note.

The Southwestern Army of Operations, as the force was dubbed, existed only briefly. Departing San Antonio in late November 1842, approximately 700 strong, the expedition set off for the Rio Grande. Somervell captured Laredo on December 8, but infighting within his force caused some to abandon the expedition. The general moved on to Guerrero and it, too, was occupied. Somervell believed he had fulfilled his orders from Houston and that nothing else could be accomplished by further endangering his force, which was short of supplies and growing smaller as men left on their own. Perhaps more important, elements within his command challenged his authority and demanded more decisive action than just raiding border towns. The embattled general broke up his force and ordered it home.

Rejecting his decision, many refused to go. Three hundred and eight Texans voted to continue the expedition, even if it meant acting without Houston's approval. The men organized themselves into five companies and elected William S. Fisher their commander. The force crossed the Rio Grande and on December 23 occupied Mier, demanding that the townspeople provide them with supplies. Told that the requested items would be delivered the next day, Fisher's men recrossed the river. Suspicions grew when the promised goods failed to materialize. The Texans learned that General Pedro de Ampudia was camped near Mier with a large body of Mexican troops. On Christmas Day, Fisher and 261 Texans marched back to Mier to collect the supplies, even if it meant fighting for them. In fact, many of the men eagerly looked forward to the chance finally to meet the enemy in battle. The Texans entered the town and occupied the houses surrounding the main plaza. Ampudia's forces attacked, and fierce fighting that lasted nearly twenty-four hours raged between the two forces. Running short of ammunition and with at least thirty troops killed and wounded, the Texans offered to surrender if they would be received as prisoners of war. Ampudia, who had suffered heavy casualties himself from the Texans ensconced in town, agreed. Fisher and his men laid down their arms and became the latest group of Texans to become prisoners of the Mexican government. Some had wanted to continue fighting but were overruled by the majority. Their warning went unheeded, and the capitulation led to one of the most dramatic events in the history of the Republic of Texas.

The captives had a long ordeal before them. Orders arrived from Mexico City for the entire command to be executed, which met with outrage and resistance by local officials. General Francisco Mejía, commander of the department of Coahuila, resigned rather than carry out the directive. The Texans were shackled and marched eastward to Matamoros, where they hoped they would be released. Instead, they were again put on the road for Mexico City. Talk of escape became more desperate as each day's march took them further from Texas. At Salado, the Texans made a bold dash against their guards, killing several before the fray was over. Armed with their captor's weapons, the prisoners reversed their course and headed north. To avoid detection, they entered the mountains that surrounded Saltillo. After a week of wandering through this dry region with no food or water, they were in no condition to resist when they stumbled into a camp of rancheros one night. Several Texans had died during the assault on the guards, several more died in the mountains from thirst and exposure, and 176 were recaptured and taken back to Salado.

A bizarre punishment awaited them at the hacienda where the escape had been made. General Nicolás Bravo, acting president in Santa Anna's absence, had demanded that they all be killed, but a compromise had been suggested by his advisers. True to the Roman definition of the term, the Texans were to be decimated: One man in ten was to die. The Texans were made to file past an earthenware container containing 176 beans. Without looking down, each man thrust his hand into the container and drew out one bean. Most of the beans were white, but seventeen (a number representing one-tenth of the captives) were black. Those men who drew white beans were spared. The seventeen men who drew black beans were led aside and allowed a brief period to prepare themselves for the fate that awaited them. The drama of the moment was captured by Robert H. Dunham, who quickly scratched out a note to his mother, telling her:

> I write you under the most awful feelings that a son ever addressed a mother, for in half an hour my [time] will be finished on earth, for I am doomed to die by the hands of the Mexicans for our late attempt to escape [by the order of] G. Santa Anna that every tenth man should be shot. We drew lots. I am one of the unfortunates. I can say nothing more. I die, I hope, with firmness. Farewell, may God bless you, and may He in this my last hour, forgive and pardon all my sins.[27]

A short time afterward the infamous deed took place in a cattle pen within hearing of the other prisoners. One of the Texans actually survived the shooting. The wounded man came to his senses that night and slipped out of the compound. Taken in by local herdsmen, he was found by Mexican soldiers and placed before a firing squad once again, this time with fatal results. One other Texan, Captain Ewen Cameron, was executed for his part in the escape, even though he had drawn a white bean. Picked out of the column of prisoners once the march to Mexico City resumed, Cameron was taken aside and shot. With Mexico's military reputation restored as the Texans marched into captivity, the stain left by the Vásquez's raid had been erased.

Houston faced the serious problem of what to do about the Texans held in Mexican prisons. He contended that the Santa Fe pioneers and Mier prisoners had acted on their own and not as official agents of the republic. Most of his countrymen, however, believed otherwise and expected him to gain their release as soon as possible. Only two options existed: rescue them by force or secure their freedom through diplomacy. Houston had already proven himself an opponent of a military action against Mexico. Negotiation, therefore, offered the only real chance.

The republic had been successful in building diplomatic ties with other nations that could help. The United States officially recognized Texas as an independent nation in March 1837. Important European governments followed suit: France in September 1839 and the Netherlands in September 1840. While Great Britain refrained from extending formal recognition, it signed a trade agreement with the republic in 1840. Several other European entities, the free cities of Lübeck, Bremen, and Hamburg, also opened trade with Texas in 1844. Without its own diplomatic representatives in Mexico, Houston depended on the republic's friends in Mexico City to intercede on behalf of the imprisoned Texans.

These forces had been at work in Mexico to free the Texans since news of the capture of the Santa Fe Pioneers. In fact, many members of the expedition had been released by order of Santa Anna in June 1842, just three months after the Vásquez Raid. Having spent ten months in captivity, these men heard the following decree that set them free:

> Tejanos! The generous Mexican nation which you offended, in reward for thousands of benefits, pardons you. In her ever-august name, I restore to you the liberty which you lost invading our territory and violating our domestic homes. March to your people and make public the fact that the Mexican people are as generous toward the defeated as brave on the battlefield. You have had evidence of their courage; witness now their magnanimity!
>
> Mexico—June 13, 1842
> Antonio López de Santa Anna[28]

Several of the Santa Fe Pioneers made it back to Texas in time to participate in the Somervell Expedition. Looking for revenge on their former captors, some participated in the attack on Mier, where they were again taken prisoner. The Texans seized by General Woll and the Mier survivors remained in prison longer than those seized in New Mexico. For some of these men, captivity lasted nearly two years. A few tired of waiting for release and staged daring escapes. But not all Texans made it home, as illness took a heavy toll. The prisoner who spent the longest time in captivity was José Antonio Navarro, who had accompanied the Santa Fe Pioneers as a commissioner empowered to open trade with New Mexico. Sentenced to life in prison for his continuing support of the Texas government, Navarro finally escaped from his imprisonment at San Juan de Ulúa at Vera Cruz and made his way home.

One diplomat who affected the release of a large number of

Texas prisoners was Waddy Thompson, U.S. minister to Mexico. He took an immediate interest in the Santa Fe Pioneers held in Mexico City, making his first official act a visit to George W. Kendall, one of the prisoners. Thompson's intervention ultimately led to the release of Kendall and most of his companions. He also interceded on behalf of the Texans captured at Mier. When informed that the recaptured men were all to be put to death, he told acting president Nicolás Bravo, "Then Sir, shoot them as soon as you choose, but let me tell you, that if you do you will at once involve in this war a much more powerful enemy than Texas."[29] Thompson and other U.S. diplomats serving in Mexico effectively alternated requests for favors and the threat of military intervention to secure the release of their former countrymen. Minister Thompson's last official act before leaving Mexico was to appeal to Santa Anna for the release of the remaining Béxar and Mier prisoners.

The renewed hostilities between Texas and Mexico reawakened U.S. interest in the region. The furor over the events at the Alamo and Goliad had died down as Americans waited to see how the Republic of Texas would fare on its own. Its shaky financial situation and frontier conditions convinced many that it would be some time before Texas blossomed into the Garden of Eden promoters promised. Mexico's conduct during the revolution and the continued warfare with Texas had created the opinion that Mexico had lost its opportunity to take its place by the United States as an equal. News of the raids by Vásquez, Canales, and Woll rallied public opinion and focused attention back on Texas and its embattled, expatriated American population.

One of Texas's most ardent and influential supporters was George W. Kendall. A native of New Hampshire, Kendall had moved to New Orleans where he became one of that city's leading newspaper publishers. He cofounded the *New Orleans Picayune* in 1837, contributing articles himself to help fill its pages. Taking a personal interest in Texas, the new republic became a frequent topic for his pen. The city's business ties with Texas boosted sales of the *Picayune*. Texas agents courted Kendall and used his paper to promote immigration, trade, and military recruiting. The urge to see Texas firsthand prompted Kendall to travel there and accompany the Santa Fe Pioneers. Thus, he shared the ordeal of the Texans on their journey to New Mexico and their subsequent capture and imprisonment. Stories of the expedition's travails that appeared in the *Picayune* were repeated by newspapers in other U.S. cities. In 1844 his account was published as *A Narrative of the Texan Santa Fé Expedition.*

Kendall painted a damning picture of his captors. Writing of one incident on the march to Mexico City, he presented this chilling tale for his readers:

> On being driven from the cart [in which he was riding], [John] McAllister declared his inability to proceed on foot. [Dimasio] Salezar drew his sword and peremptorily ordered him to hurry on, . . . "Forward!" said Salezar, now wrought up to a pitch of phrensy. "Forward or I'll shoot you on the spot." "Then shoot!" replied McAllister, throwing off his blanket and exposing his manly breast, "and the quicker the better!" Salezar took him at his word, and a single ball sent as brave a man as ever trod the earth to eternity! His ears were then cut off, his shirt and pantaloon stripped from him, and his body throw by the roadside as food for wolves![30]

Several elements of the scene described by Kendall horrified the American public. The severed ears were used by the captors as an accounting measure to prove to their superiors that no prisoners had escaped. The man had been denied a Christian burial. Not least, an act of bravery had been rebuked and repaid with cruelty. These things did not sit well with American readers.

The Mier prisoners also had their own chroniclers. One was Thomas Jefferson Green, an ardent foe of Sam Houston. Green had come to Texas during the revolution and received a commission as a brigadier general in return for recruiting volunteers from the United States. He and his men docked at Velasco in June 1836 to find that Santa Anna was about to be sent back to Mexico by Texas officials. He demanded that the Mexican general and his staff be landed, thereby derailing the Treaty of Velasco. Always involved on the political front of the republic, Green publicly castigated Houston for not waging war against Mexico after that country's incursions into Texas. Accompanying Somervell's expedition to the Rio Grande, he continued on to Mier with Fisher's column. His account of the Mier Expedition was published in 1845 as *A Journal of the Texian Expedition against Mier.* He did not wait for release but escaped from Perote Castle with a number of other Texans.

Green described more scenes of Mexican cruelty for American readers. Writing of the moments leading up to the execution of the seventeen Texans at Salado, he told of the cool reaction of one of the condemned men:

> Several of our men were permitted to visit the unfortunates previous to the execution, to receive their dying requests. Poor Major [James D.] Cocke, when he drew the first fatal bean, held it up between his forefinger and thumb, and with a smile of contempt, said, "Boys, I told you so; I never failed in my life to draw a prize;" and then said to Judge Gibson, "Well, judge, say to my friends that I died in grace." The judge, much affected at this last sad parting, showed it from his tears. The major replied, "They only rob me of forty years," and then sat down and wrote a sensible and dignified letter of remonstrance to General Waddy Thompson, the United States minister in Mexico; and knowing that his remains would be robbed of his clothing after his death, drew off his pantaloons, handed them to his surviving comrades, and died in his underclothes.[31]

Both Kendall and Green presented the Texan prisoners in stark contrast to their Mexican captors, portraying the former as noble heroes and the latter as contemptible fiends. Americans added Santa Fe, Mier, and Perote Castle to the growing list of Mexican atrocities to be avenged.

Although Texas military exploits on land failed to live up to their expectations, Texans could boast of real successes at sea. The Texas Navy owed its existence to the action of the General Council in November 1835. At the same time it created a regular army and named Houston as its commander, the legislative body also voted to commission a naval force to defend its shores. The purchase of four ships—*Brutus, Independence, Invincible,* and *Liberty*—completed Texas's first fleet. The ships performed valuable service in spring 1836, capturing Mexican supplies and battling its navy on the gulf. Ships in the age of sail had short life spans, though, due to rot and natural phenomena such as storms and underwater hazards. Texas ships faced an additional danger—creditors. By fall 1837, Texas had lost its entire fleet: *Liberty,* seized for nonpayment of debt at New Orleans in July 1836; *Independence,* captured by the Mexican Navy in a fight off Galveston in April 1836; *Invincible,* run aground near Galveston in August 1837; and *Brutus,* lost in a storm in September 1837. Thus ended the first Texas Navy.

The Texas Navy, like the regular army, was revived by Lamar. Legislation to rebuild the fleet had gone unenforced by Houston, who extended his cost-cutting philosophy to include the Texas Navy. According to his reasoning, a navy was too expensive and would only deepen the conflict between Texas and Mexico. The new fleet acquired in 1839 eventually numbered seven ships: *Archer, Austin, San Jacinto, San Antonio, San Bernard, Wharton,* and *Zavala.* Although the first six ships were propelled by sail, the seventh was a steamer. Like the first fleet, these ships extended Texas's presence into the gulf and along the Mexican coast. Still, as Houston had warned, keeping the navy provisioned and prepared required funds that the treasury lacked. In 1841 a plan arose to rent the Texas Navy to the Mexican state of Yucatán, then in revolt against the centralist government in Mexico City. Thus, not only were the navy's expenses paid; the arrangement also allowed Texas to assist fellow republicans in their struggle for independence.

Despite its successes, the second Texas Navy also met an inglorious end. On taking office for the second time, Houston ordered the navy back to port and into mothball. Edwin Ward Moore, appointed commodore by Lamar, refused to bring the fleet in and used his own credit to keep the navy going while he worked to renew the navy's rental arrangement with Yucatán. Houston labeled Commodore Moore and his men pirates and declared that any nation had the right to bring the outlaws to justice. In July 1843, Moore brought the fleet into the naval yard at Galveston amid the cheers of its residents. The nation's adulation failed to prevent Houston from discharging Moore and breaking up the fleet. The *San Jacinto* and *San Antonio* had been lost at sea in 1840 and 1842, respectively. The *Zavala,* which had fallen into disrepair, was scrapped. Of the remaining ships, *Wharton, Austin, San Bernard,* and *Archer,* only the last-named vessel was still fit enough to be accepted by the U.S. Navy following the transfer of the navy's assets after annexation in 1845. An interesting side note to the Texas Navy's demise is that the Colt revolving pistols purchased for it were reissued to Texas Rangers such as John C. Hays, in whose hands they became formidable weapons against the republic's enemies on land.

Beginning in 1843 relations between Texas and Mexico entered a period of relative peace, if peace is defined as solely the absence of hostilities. The governments of both nations agreed to an armistice as a prelude to negotiations that would settle their difficulties once and for all. The armistice was signed on February 15, 1844, at the town of Sabinas on the Rio Grande. Santa Anna, who took office again after the truce was approved, revoked the arrangement, claiming that the Texans were not serious about negotiating a lasting peace.[32] By then, however, developments outside of Texas and Mexico were shaping the region's future.

NOTES

1. H. Yoakum, *History of Texas* (New York: Redfield, 1856), 2:526–528.
2. Amelia Williams and Eugene C. Barker, eds., *The Writings of Sam Houston, 1813–1863* (Austin: University of Texas Press, 1938–1943), 1: 448–452.
3. Ibid.
4. Charles A. Gulick Jr. and Katherine Elliot, eds., *The Papers of Mirabeau Buonaparte Lamar* (Austin: A. C. Baldwin, 1920–1927), 2:316.
5. Ibid.
6. Ibid., 2:348–349, 354–355.
7. Ibid.
8. Ibid., 2:321–322.
9. Gulick Jr. and Elliot, eds., *Papers of Mirabeau Buonaparte Lamar,* 1:352.
10. "Treaty of Tehuacana, Creek, October 9, 1844," in Ernest Wallace, David M. Vigness, and George B. Ward, eds., *Documents of Texas History,* 2d ed. (Austin: State House Press, 1994), 144–146.
11. H. P. N. Gammel, *The Laws of Texas, 1822–1897* (Austin: Gammel Book Company, 1898), 1:1193–1194.
12. Miguel A. Sánchez Lamego, *The Second Mexican-Texas War, 1841–1843* (Hillsboro, TX: Hill Junior College Press, 1972), 75.
13. Ibid., 82.
14. Ibid., 83.
15. Ibid., 89.
16. Ibid.
17. Ibid., 90.
18. Ibid.
19. Ibid., 98.
20. Ibid., 31–32.
21. Eugene C. Barker, "Texas Revolutionary Army," *Quarterly of the Texas State Historical Association* (April 1906), 241.
22. John H. Jenkins, ed., *The Papers of the Texas Revolution: 1835–1836,* (Austin: Presidial Press, 1973), 3:369–370.
23. Gammel, *Laws of Texas,* 1:1094–1111.
24. Ibid., 1:1114–1128.
25. John F. Callam, *The Military Laws of the United States* (Philadelphia: G. W. Childs, 1863), 95–100, 108–110.
26. Gammel, *Laws of Texas,* 2:236–237; 419–420, 516, 544, 974, 1171.
27. Sam W. Haynes, *Soldiers of Misfortune: The Somervell and Mier Expe-*

ditions (Austin: University of Texas Press, 1990), 125. Robert H. Dunham's letter is part of The Alamo Collection, San Antonio, Texas.

28. "Santa Anna's Proclamation Freeing Texan Prisoners," The Alamo Collection, San Antonio, Texas.

29. Waddy Thompson, *Recollections of Mexico* (New York: Wiley and Putnam, 1846), 73–74. For a list of the Texan prisoners and their deposition, see Thomas J. Green, *Journal of the Texian Expedition against Mier* (1845; Austin: Steck Company, 1935), 437–450.

30. Geo. Wilkins Kendall, *Narrative of the Texan Santa Fé Expedition,* (New York: Harper and Brothers, 1844), 1:393–394.

31. Green, *Journal of the Texian Expedition against Mier,* 171–172.

32. Sanchez Lamego, *The Second Mexican-Texas War,* 53–55.

CHAPTER THREE

ACT ONE
Annexation and the Coming of War

Walk in my tall haired Indian gal,
    Your hand, my star-eyed Texas,
You're welcome in our White House hall,
    Tho' Mexy's hounds would vex us;
Come on and take some Johnny cake,
    With lasses snug an' coodle,
For that an' Independence make,
    A full blood Yankee Doodle.
—"Uncle Sam's Song to Miss Texas"
The National Songster (ca. 1848)

THE ANNEXATION OF Texas by the United States seemed a foregone conclusion to many Texans and Americans. One speculator in Texas lands prior to the Texas Revolution even declared, "When we consider that this land lies contiguous to the United States, of which it will probably soon form a part,"[1] to comfort investors who might be worried about risking their money on a foreign venture. Thus, Mexicans had always been suspicious of American expansion, with good reason.

Ever since the dawn of the nineteenth century, Americans had pushed steadily westward, regardless of the claims to territory by other nations. The justification for this aggressive migration had its roots in the concept of Manifest Destiny. While discounted by some modern historians as merely a justification to seize land, Manifest Destiny was very real to post–Revolutionary War citizens of the new republic called the United States of America. Speaking of Manifest Destiny in 1996, Mexican historian Miguel González Quiroga cautioned, "It is dangerous to underestimate the power of an idea, especially one that captures the imagination of a people."[2] The idea definitely captured Americans' imagination.

Simply stated, early Americans believed that God intended for them and their offspring to inhabit the continent of North America. The concept of Manifest Destiny had several basic components. First, the men and women of the United States held the conviction that they were God's chosen people. The notion was linked to the Puritan belief that their New World settlement would be a "shining city on a hill" and serve as an example to others. The hardships overcome by the early settlers, in addition to the monumental split with Great Britain, were viewed by early Americans as evidence that God had indeed shown favor on the young nation. God intended for Americans, because of their supposed superior institutions and character, to spread across the land as a testimony to His power and generosity. Those in the way had two choices—convert or move out of the way. Anyone too slow in choosing would be pushed aside.

Critics of Manifest Destiny claim that racism lay at its heart. "Race," however, for early Americans was defined much more broadly than as just the color of one's skin. The term incorporated ethnicity, religion, and government. There is no doubt that white Americans considered themselves superior to Africans, Indians, Mexicans, and other people of color. Not that far removed in time from the Protestant Reformation and the brutal wars between Protestant and Catholic nations, early Americans also had an innate mistrust of and disdain for anything papal. With its hierarchical links to Rome, Catholicism was considered blatantly undemocratic and a threat to republican principles. Moreover, these people were motivated by the ideals of the American Revolution and considered themselves revolutionaries in the same vein as their parents and grandparents had been. The evangelical movement known as the Second Great Awakening, which swept across the country in the early nineteenth century, reinforced the idea of free will and the importance of the individual. Revolutionary fervor and evangelical zeal combined to create a fierce belief in republicanism. Americans were intensely proud that they were citizens in a federal republic and not subjects of a monarch. The ideological underpinning of Manifest Destiny ran deep and shaped the way early Americans viewed their world.

The children of Washington took seriously their perceived charge from God to go forth and be fruitful. Land equaled livelihood in an age of agrarianism. Occupying new territory served a twofold purpose. First, it aided the spread of republicanism and, second, it provided room for these republicans to perpetuate their "race." Although many modern scholars have depicted the westward movement as a massive land grab, this interpretation is extremely narrow and fails to take into consideration the ideological and intellectual framework of the time.

Many Americans believed that Mexico had failed to live up to its promise and therefore deserved whatever fate lay in store for it. One American who voiced this opinion was Captain Robert Anderson, the future commander of Union forces at Fort Sumter, South Carolina. Writing from central Mexico in May 1847, Anderson proclaimed, "Poor deluded nation—the people are not fit for self-government, and we are, perhaps, instruments intended to open this country to the world and finally establish enlightened and free government in it."[3] His comments echo those made by Americans for years prior to the Mexican War.

Although the term "Manifest Destiny" has traditionally been associated with the decade of the 1840s, recent scholarship has shown that the processes it embodied had been at work since at least the early years of the American Republic, if not before. Americans had eyed Spanish territory prior to ever setting foot on Texas soil. Conditioned as we are to think of Spain's territory as consisting only of the land that now makes up the American Southwest, it is easy to forget that much of the land adjacent to the Gulf Coast east of the Mississippi River was acknowledged as Spanish until the enactment of the Adams-Onís Treaty. Likewise, the vast area that composed the Louisiana Purchase was controlled by Spain from 1763 until it was reclaimed by the French in 1800. Thus, there was much Spanish land to covet. To Thomas Jefferson and many of his contemporaries, Americans had the obligation, if not the divine right, to evict the land's aristocratic and Catholic landlords. The mysterious Burr Conspiracy of 1806 and repeated American excursions into East and West Florida between 1810 and 1818 are early expressions of Manifest Destiny.

American designs on Texas emerged shortly after 1800. By then some of the larger continental issues facing the United States had been resolved, leaving its citizens free to consider their future. Most

important, the Louisiana Purchase had removed the buffer between the Vice Royalty of New Spain and the United States, creating
jumping-off points for men willing to venture into this foreign land.
In 1806, Lieutenant Colonel Simón de Herrera and Brigadier General James Wilkinson, local military commanders in Texas and Louisiana, respectively, settled on a plan to prevent conflict between
their two countries by proclaiming as neutral ground a narrow strip
along the east bank of the Sabine River. Although it prevented outright hostilities between the United States and Spain, this no-man's
land became a haven for rebels and filibusters. After the suppression
of Father Hidalgo's 1810 insurrection, Mexican revolutionaries fleeing royal wrath took advantage of the refuge that the neutral ground
offered.

The mix of republicans (Mexican and American) in the neutral
ground proved volatile. One member of Hidalgo's revolutionary
circle, José Bernardo Maximiliano Gutiérrez de Lara, had been sent
to the United States to secure aid for the revolt. Making his way
to Washington, DC, he presented his plan directly to Secretary of
State James Monroe. Encouraged but denied direct assistance, Gutiérrez returned to Louisiana, where he and Augustus William Magee, a graduate of the U.S. Military Academy, assembled an expedition intended to free Texas from Spanish rule. Magee, who resigned
his officer's commission in the U.S. Army in order to accompany the
expedition, was named military commander of the combined American and Mexican force, while Gutiérrez retained overall leadership
of the Republican Army of the North.

The invasion began on August 12, 1812, when the expedition
crossed the Sabine River into Texas. Soon Nacogdoches and La Bahía (Goliad) were occupied by Magee's troops. Lieutenant Colonel
Simón de Herrera reacted to the incursion by marching on La Bahía
and besieging the republicans, who in November had taken possession of the old presidio (fort), along the San Antonio River. The royalist commander lifted the siege four months later when the republicans still had not been defeated or captured. During the siege,
Magee died under mysterious circumstances, and Major Samuel
Kemper was named his successor. On March 29, 1813, republican
and royalist forces clashed several miles east of San Antonio on
Salado Creek. Herrera was routed, and Gutiérrez and Kemper en-

tered San Antonio, taking up quarters in a former mission, by then known as the Alamo. The brutal executions by Gutiérrez of Governor Manuel Salcedo, Herrera, and several other high-ranking royalists caused many Americans participating in the venture to abandon the expedition in disgust. Soon Gutiérrez would also be removed from the scene.

Secretary Monroe followed the progress of the expedition into Texas. Because the United States could not overtly take part in the affair, he relied on more discreet means by which to influence the venture. Captain William Shaler, working through the State Department, was assigned to assist Gutiérrez and kept the American government informed of the revolutionary's movements. Officials in the United States had recruited another revolutionary, Cuban-born José Álvarez de Toledo de Dubois, and groomed him as Gutiérrez's replacement. The ouster occurred at San Antonio in August 1813. Toledo and Shaler picked Major Henry Perry to command the republican army. Perry faced a serious challenge from the royalists, who had sent General José Joaquín de Arredondo y Mioño with a force strong enough to crush the rebels. On August 18, 1813, Arredondo met and overwhelmed Perry's joint American and Mexican command south of San Antonio near the Medina River. So disastrous was the defeat for the republicans that it effectively ended any hopes for further success. The royalists captured nine pieces of artillery and nearly 1,000 firearms besides killing or capturing nearly all of Perry's 1,400 men.

In what some historians have described as a precursor to the mass executions of Texans in 1836, Arredondo ordered 327 republicans put to death in the days after his victory on the Medina. Informing his superior of the battle, Arredondo wrote: "The greater part [of Toledo's force] were Americans, among them being the son of General Wilkinson, Colonel Menchaca, and many other officers of the rabble. The field was covered with many wounded as has been verified by numerous reports. Their arms, their park of artillery, prisoners (who have been executed as just punishment for their crimes), and whatever else was found were seized."[4]

In the same report, he stated of prisoners that "those deserving death, on account of their crimes, were shot." He also praised the conduct of his officers and men, singling out a junior officer for his "great bravery." For Antonio López de Santa Anna, the young man to whom he referred, the Battle of the Medina and its aftermath may have been an indelible lesson in how to treat rebels and filibusters.

Although Arredondo claimed that most the dead were American filibusters, he exacted a heavy toll on the Tejano population of San Antonio and La Bahía. Mexican republicans fled for their lives, trying to reach the neutral ground ahead of royalist cavalry being sent to punish them. At least two who made it to safety, José Francisco Ruiz and José Antonio Navarro, would again become revolutionaries and even signers of the Texas Declaration of Independence in 1836. Family members of Mexican republicans were imprisoned and forced to work for the royalist soldiers. The disastrous Gutiérrez-Magee Expedition set back the economy of Texas for years to come. It also significantly reduced the population in the region at a time when Spain needed all the inhabitants it could muster, making the colonization of Texas imperative and paving the way for American colonists.

One veteran of the Gutiérrez-Magee Expedition returned to Texas to carry on the fight against the royalists. Henry Perry, commander of the republican forces at the Battle of the Medina, had joined General Francisco Xavier Mina's 1817 campaign against Tamaulipas. Dissatisfied with Mina's progress, Perry left the expedition and marched with forty-three volunteers to La Bahía. The royalist garrison refused to surrender, choosing instead to fight. Perry withdrew but, on June 19, 1817, he and most of his men were killed when the two sides clashed.

One last attempt to tear Texas away from Spain occurred after Luis de Onís had negotiated a treaty guaranteeing Spanish claim to the region. An expedition led by James Long failed to establish a stronghold in Texas, but the adventure did give one member of the expedition, Long's wife Jane, the appellation of "The Mother of Texas" (or at least Anglo Texas). Long was taken as a prisoner to Mexico City, where he died under suspicious circumstances. Jane Long found success in Texas as a valued member of Stephen F. Austin's colony once it was established.

〜 Some of Sam Houston's contemporaries as well as some historians surmised that he had actually been sent to Texas by his mentor, Andrew Jackson, to bring Texas into the Union. Old Hickory had made known his desire to acquire Texas when he authorized the U.S. minister to Mexico, Joel Poinsett, to offer up to $5 million for the province's purchase. Poinsett, who outraged many Mexicans when he meddled in their nation's politics by openly siding with the liberals, was recalled before he could accomplish this task. His successor, Anthony Butler, operated under the same instructions from Jackson. Proponents of the Jackson-Houston conspiracy contend that, unable to purchase Texas, Jackson sent his protégé to secure it for him by precipitating a revolution. No hard evidence exists of this supposed conspiracy, however, and it appears that Houston came to Texas like so many others, drawn by the potential it offered. The theory also presupposes that Houston was the prime author of the Texas Revolution when, in fact, he was only one actor in an ensemble cast. Nonetheless, ample evidence reveals that Houston and his compatriots still felt a strong connection to the United States.

The annexation issue arose as soon as Texas gained its independence from Mexico. In September 1836, Texans went to the polls to formalize the gains they had made in their revolt against the Mexican government. Two questions dealt specifically with the process of institutionalizing the new republic: ratifying the constitution presented at Washington-on-the-Brazos and choosing its leaders. A third question, however, was put before voters. Did they desire annexation to the United States? The results were overwhelmingly in favor of joining the Union, as 3,277 ballots were cast in favor of annexation as compared with 91 opposing votes. Existence as an independent nation was not the first choice of most Texans.

Many decisions of national importance during the early history of the United States hinged on the issue of slavery. Slavery, at one time legal in all the thirteen British colonies, had gradually been excluded from the Northern states. The reason for its decline in that region was as much economic as it was moral: An adequate workforce meant slavery was not needed. Throughout the early 1800s, the United States split into two distinct regions: the North, often called the free states, and the South, usually referred to as the slave states. Because each region feared that the other would gain the upper hand in the U.S. Congress, the issue of admitting new states proved highly volatile.

To eliminate potential conflict, the U.S. Congress often resorted to compromise whenever the slavery issue came before them. In one of the first examples of this practice, the delegates who constructed the U.S. Constitution agreed to halt the importation of African slaves after 1808 in exchange for counting slaves already in the country as three-fifths of a person, for the purpose of determining representation in the House of Representatives. In the years after the American Revolution, settlers had spilled over the Appalachian Mountains, filling up the Old Northwest and the Old Southwest. Divided by the Ohio River, the area north of the river was declared "slave free" by the Northwest Ordinance (1787), while no such law prevented owners from taking their human property with them into the area to the south. The organization of these two territories into states progressed at a steady pace, prompting a contest of sorts to ensure that one side did not gain a permanent advantage over the other by creating either a majority for the free or slave states.

The question of parity and compromise was severely tested in 1819 when Missouri Territory petitioned for admittance to the Union as a slave state. The time had come to decide whether slavery would be allowed to exist in the land comprising the old Louisiana Purchase. Residents of Missouri had included a proslavery clause in their proposed constitution. Opponents of slavery vigorously fought against Missouri's admittance, afraid that it would establish a precedent and open the area west of the Mississippi River to what was known as "the peculiar institution." Adherents of slavery declared that the Constitution guaranteed the right to transport and hold personal property in any place in the Union even if that property were human. The debate became more and more heated until a solution emerged that seemed to offer both sides a way to declare victory. Passed in 1820 and called the Missouri Compromise, the agreement had several parts. First, Missouri was allowed into the Union as a slave state. Second, Maine was admitted as a free state to preserve the balance of power between the two sections. The addition of these two new states meant that there would be eleven slave and eleven free states. Third, the Louisiana Purchase was divided along the line of latitude 36 degrees 30 minutes, with the stipulation that land north of the line would forever be closed to slavery, while in the territory south of it the institution would be permitted. With the passage of the Missouri Compromise, the question of slavery's extension into new territory was supposed to be settled.

The Texas Revolution reopened the debate. Many Southerners

believed that Texas had actually been a part of the Louisiana Purchase and that it had been given away by Secretary of State John Quincy Adams in the Adams-Onís Treaty of 1819. According to this extreme interpretation, Americans had a right to Texas and the revolution of 1835–36 was merely returning the land to its former owners. Also, one look at a map of the United States in 1821 showed that the distribution of the Louisiana Purchase according to the Missouri Compromise had offered the free states greater opportunities for growth. South of 36 degrees 30 minutes latitude lay Arkansas Territory, from which was soon carved Indian Territory, a large area of land off-limits to settlement by non-Indians. From north of the line would come the future states of Iowa, Minnesota, Kansas, Colorado, North Dakota, South Dakota, Montana, Washington, and Oregon. While most of these states did not enter the Union until after the Civil War, new boundary lines demonstrate the extent of the territory into which slave owners were forbidden to carry their human property after passage of the Missouri Compromise. It also dramatically demonstrates why Texas became so important to the future of American slavery. Where else besides Texas could slave owners acquire more land in the 1820s and 1830s?

The first government of independent Mexico to address the slavery issue was that of Emperor Agustín de Iturbide. On January 4, 1823, an imperial law on colonization stated, "After the publication of the law, there can be no sale or purchase of slaves which may be introduced into the empire. The children of slaves born in the empire shall be free at fourteen years of age."[5] While the law did not declare an outright ban on slavery, it planned for the eventual abolition of the institution by cutting off the supply from outside Mexico as well as mandating the emancipation of children born into slavery. The Mexican Constitution of 1824 did not address the slavery issue. Thus, no prohibition prevented Austin from issuing regulations regarding slavery in his own colony, ordinances that dealt mainly with runaways, slave stealing, and other common issues related to the institution.

Later legislation and decrees addressed, but did not necessarily clarify, the question of slavery in Texas. The state legislature of Coahuila and Texas at Saltillo passed a March 24, 1825, colonization law stating, "In respect to the introduction of slaves, the new settlers shall subject themselves to the laws that are now, and hereafter shall

be established on the subject."[6] On March 11, 1827, the state constitution was ratified. Article 13 of the document stated, "From and after the promulgation of the constitution in the capital of each district, no one shall be born a slave in the state, and after six months
the introduction of slaves under any pretext shall not be permitted."[7] On September 15, 1827, the governor of the state issued Decree No. 18, which called for officials to establish lists of slaves
within their districts so that each bondsman could be tracked and
his or her condition verified.[8]

Although these laws make it appear that state officials would
not tolerate slavery in Texas, a new law actually made it possible for
slavery to continue and even grow. Responding to concerns that
Americans would not come to Texas unless they could bring slaves,
on May 5, 1828, the governor issued Decree No. 56, which acknowledged labor contracts with bondsmen as valid and binding agree-
ments, citing the need "attending to the deficiency of working men
to give activity to agriculture and the other arts."[9] Using the practice of debt peonage as a model, the law allowed slave owners in the
United States to take their slaves before a magistrate before entering
Texas and to have their human property declared indentured servants. Thus, slave owners continued to enter Texas with their property with only minor inconveniences.

The threat to slavery worried its supporters both in the United
States and Texas because at any time the Mexican government could
harden its stance against the institution. Their fears were justified
because on the eve of the nineteenth anniversary of Hidalgo's revolt,
September 15, 1829, liberal President Vicente Guerrero announced
the emancipation of all slaves within the republic. Faced with the
possibility of devastating financial losses and the curtailment of immigration to Texas, slave owners petitioned the governor and legislature at Saltillo for help. On December 2, 1829, Guerrero exempted
Texas from the emancipation decree. The institution seemed safe
once more.

The situation again changed when the Mexican government unexpectedly closed immigration to Texas from the United States.
While Article 10 of the Law of April 6, 1830, promised that "no
change shall be made with respect to the slaves now in the states," it
admonished that "the federal government and government of each
state shall most strictly enforce the colonization laws and prevent

the further introduction of slaves."[10] With no slaves allowed in from the outside via immigration and a crackdown on smuggling, slavery's days in Texas seemed numbered.

The insistence on the part of the colonists that Texas remain open to slavery gave the Mexican officials and abolitionists in the United States a valuable tool in the war of popular opinion. How could the colonists be fighting for liberty if they supported the practice of keeping others in perpetual bondage? The Mexican government claimed the conflict was not a revolution at all but an attempt to tear Texas away so slavery could be protected. The abolitionist press in the United States expressed the view that the push into Texas had been a conspiracy by the "Southern Slave Power" to extend the institution across the continent. The attacks on Texans' motives did not end with the establishment of the Republic of Texas in 1836, as its constitution promised to protect the institution of slavery, forbidding the Texas Republic's lawmakers from passing any legislation that would prohibit U.S. immigrants from bringing their slaves with them.[11]

The slavery issue proved to be the greatest impediment to annexation that Texas faced. While some doubted that the Constitution allowed for the incorporation of a foreign nation into the Union, the antislavery faction in the United States feared that granting Texas statehood would make the institution even harder to eradicate and, therefore, they mounted an all-out effort to block annexation. The early 1830s marked a noticeable increase in antislavery activity. The first edition of William Lloyd Garrison's antislavery newspaper, *The Liberator,* appeared in 1831. The following year saw the formation of the New England Anti-Slavery Society, which gave rise to the American Anti-Slavery Society in 1833. American abolitionists received encouragement from abroad when, in 1833, Great Britain abolished slavery within the British Empire. Abolitionist writers followed up these successes by attempting to flood the slave states with antislavery newspapers, pamphlets, and correspondence. Southerners, who feared that the agitation would spawn such slave insurrections as Virginia's 1831 Nat Turner Revolt, believed the mass mailings were a threat to civil order and demanded that the federal government take action to prevent the use of the mail in this manner. Some postmasters refused to deliver the abolitionist material, explaining that it was too incendiary to distribute. Abolitionists also targeted the U.S. Congress, sending petitions that damned the practice of slavery. The debate over the petitions bogged down business and further divided the U.S. Congress along sectional lines. In response to the petitions, the U.S. Congress passed a series of "gag rules" designed to silence the controversy by tabling without reading all such petitions that were received. The order was in place from 1836 though 1844. Into this boiling political cauldron the question of Texas's future was thrown.

Sam Houston relayed Texas's desire to join the Union shortly after voters expressed an overwhelming preference for annexation. His representative in Washington, DC, William H. Wharton, had been an important political and diplomatic figure in the Texas Revolution. President Jackson, who had seemed so eager to obtain Texas, now urged caution, apparently wanting the U.S. Congress to take the lead in annexation. His hesitation may have stemmed in part from the fact that his second term in office had nearly expired, and he knew that he would not be in a position to oversee the sensitive process of securing statehood. Also, the danger of engaging the country in a war was real, because Mexico still hoped that the situation in Texas was only temporary and that control over the wayward territory would soon be reestablished. On March 3, 1837, however, Jackson extended official U.S. recognition to the breakaway republic and nominated Alcée La Branche of Louisiana as chargé d'affaires to the Republic of Texas. By August 1837, Wharton had been replaced by Memucan Hunt, who made the actual offer of annexation to the United States. Jackson's successor, Martin Van Buren of New York, was less supportive of the Texas issue than had been his predecessor and rejected the offer. Hunt received the following explanation: First, the Constitution did not allow the annexation of another nation and, second, as Texas and Mexico were technically still at war, annexation would possibly involve the United States and other nations in the conflict. Thus, Texas's first attempt to join the Union ended in failure.

More was at stake, though, than issues of constitutionality or even the possibility of war with a foreign power. The slavery debate, which Texas came to epitomize in the 1830s and 1840s, threatened to split the fabric of American politics and, by extension, the nation. Political factions had polarized into two parties, the Democrats and the Whigs. The first was the party forged by supporters of Andrew

Jackson. The second formed in opposition to the Democrats. Both parties had members throughout the nation, but it was possible for such national coalitions to exist only as long as divisive issues such as slavery were kept from driving Americans into sectional camps. Thus, Northern and Southern Democrats were able to cooperate on issues that they both supported just as Northern and Southern Whigs cooperated on issues they favored. Party leaders such as Van Buren sensed that the Texas question threatened the traditional national alliances and thus was too dangerous even to debate.

Rebuffed, Houston did not press the issue. The offer remained in effect until 1838 when he ordered it officially withdrawn. His successor to the presidency, Mirabeau Buonaparte Lamar, had no desire to see Texas join the Union and therefore took no action toward annexation, preferring instead to expand the republic. The disastrous Santa Fe Expedition and the calamities that followed left Texas in a poor bargaining position when Houston returned to office in 1841.

In December 1842 the possibility of annexation was once again the topic of conversation in Washington, DC. President Van Buren had lost his reelection bid to William Henry Harrison, the Whigs' answer to Old Hickory. The victory was short-lived because Harrison died of pneumonia, contracted while delivering his inaugural address in a cold rain. He was succeeded by John Tyler, a political anomaly. A Virginian, Tyler had fallen out with the Jacksonians and therefore was added to the ticket with Harrison to provide balance. No one ever expected him to become president, leading his detractors to refer to him as "His Accidentcy" when Harrison's unexpected death placed him in the White House. A Southern Democrat, Tyler was much more receptive to the idea of annexation than had been either Van Buren of New York or Harrison of Ohio. Instructed by Houston, Texas's Chargé d'Affaires Isaac Van Zandt discussed annexation with Tyler, who offered encouragement but warned that many in the U.S. Congress still opposed the union of the two republics. Although the situation had shifted in Texas's favor, annexation was by no means certain.

Houston commenced a high-stakes diplomatic game that involved the United States, Great Britain, France, and Mexico as unwitting players. Withdrawing this second offer of annexation, Houston hinted that Great Britain and France planned to broker peace between Texas and Mexico, thereby placing his republic on a strong footing and making any union with the United States unnecessary. Many Americans still feared and loathed Great Britain and abhorred the idea that it might come to Texas's aid. The thought that Texas might make a deal with such a hereditary enemy of the United States as John Bull was inconceivable to many Americans. Moreover, such a pact would likely strengthen Great Britain's standing in the region and put her closer to controlling California's deep-water ports. U.S. slave owners realized that in exchange for its help, Great Britain would demand the curtailment of slavery. By September 1843, Van Zandt was able to report to Houston that Tyler and his cabinet members had approached him with news that they believed the Senate finally was ready to support a treaty of annexation linking the United States and Texas. Houston, anticipating that such a link would likely provoke a hostile reaction from Mexico, asked Van Zandt to ensure that Tyler knew that the United States would have to move quickly to protect Texas in case annexation was effected.

Proponents of annexation, both in Texas and the United States, believed that it could be accomplished by treaty. Houston sent J. Pinckney Henderson to assist Van Zandt in Washington, DC, in working out the terms of the agreement. On April 12, 1844, representatives of both nations signed an annexation treaty admitting Texas to the Union. Its preamble stated,

> The people of Texas having, at the time of adopting their Constitution, expressed, by an almost unanimous vote, their desire to be incorporated into the Union of the United States, and being still desirous of the same with equal unanimity, in order to provide more effectually for their security and prosperity; the United States, actuated solely by the desire to add to their own security and prosperity, and to meet the wishes of the Government and people of Texas, have determined to accomplish, by treaty, objects so important to their mutual and permanent welfare.[12]

Texas would turn over its military posts, navy, and other public property to the United States; its citizens would have the rights guaranteed U.S. citizens; valid titles and claims would be recognized; records of the Texas Land Office would be turned over pending decisions regarding public land; the United States would assume Texas's governmental debt up to the sum of $10 million; Texas law would remain in effect during the transition from republic to state; and commissioners appointed by the president of the United States would oversee the exchange of property and settlement of claims. Six months were allowed for ratification of the treaty by both parties and for the exchange of signed copies. When it came up for vote on June 8, 1844, the promised support failed to materialize, and the treaty failed by a vote of thirty-five to sixteen. Texas had been rejected a second time.

The explanation for the treaty's defeat lay in the fact that the U.S. presidential election was only months away. Tyler was essentially without a party and therefore had no vehicle by which to pursue reelection. The obvious choice for the Democratic nomination was Van Buren, who along with his supporters believed that the office was rightfully his. The Whigs relied on party faithful Henry Clay as their champion. Both candidates endeavored to avoid the annexation issue, knowing that whatever comments they made would naturally offend one side or the other and cost them votes. A letter by Clay finally appeared in print in which he stated that he opposed Texas's immediate annexation to the Union. His supporters interpreted this to mean that he opposed the annexation treaty before the Senate. Van Buren, also in a letter, indicated that Texas and Mexico must make peace before annexation was possible. Thus, both candidates announced their opposition to the annexation treaty and paid the political consequences. Although the candidates' supporters in the Senate followed their dictates and blocked annexation, American voters were yet to have their say.

Both parties held their nominating conventions in the midst of the controversy swirling around Texas. Meeting in Baltimore, Maryland, in May 1844 the Whigs unanimously nominated Henry Clay for president and Theodore Frelinghuysen as his running mate. The Democrats also met in Baltimore later that month to choose their candidates, but their convention was far from routine. Many Democratic delegates had developed doubts about Van Buren's suitability for the office because of his stance on Texas and other issues. Southerners wanted a more sympathetic candidate. When Van Buren failed to win the nomination on the first ballot by the required two-thirds vote needed, supporters knew he was in trouble. Another name began to be uttered by the delegates—James Knox Polk. A Tennessean like Houston, Polk's mentor had also been Andrew Jackson. "Young Hickory," as he was called, was thought to hold ideological views similar to those of Jackson and was not squeamish about expanding the boundaries of the United States. Borrowing a term from the racetrack for a horse that unexpectedly emerges from behind to beat the favorite, the delegates labeled Polk a dark-horse candidate, because his emergence seemed so miraculous. Actually, much maneuvering had taken place behind the scenes to push Polk's candidacy forward. When the convention ended, Polk had the Democratic nomination, backed by running mate George M. Dallas of Pennsylvania to even out the ticket by appealing to Northern voters.

Polk's campaign was designed to appeal to expansionists in both the North and South. To Northerners, Polk cried, "Fifty-four forty or fight!" The slogan referred to the dispute between the United States and Great Britain over Oregon Country. Both countries had established a claim to the region dating back to the last century. In 1778 British explorer Captain James Cook visited the area during one of his Pacific Ocean voyages. In 1792 American sea captain Robert Gray discovered the mouth of the Columbia River, while later that year another Englishman, George Vancouver, sailed his ship upstream some distance before turning back. The American explorers Lewis and Clark wintered near the mouth of the Columbia River in 1805–06. Both countries established commercial endeavors in the region built on the fur trade: John Jacob Astor's Pacific Fur Company (U.S.) and the Hudson's Bay Company (British). In 1818 the United States and Britain agreed to fix the forty-ninth parallel from the Great Lakes to the Rocky Mountains as the boundary between the United States and British Canada. Oregon Country, the land west of the Rockies to the Pacific Ocean, was to be jointly occupied by citizens of both countries. While the treaty did not provide a permanent solution, it prevented further hostilities between these two old enemies by delaying a decision on the matter.

Several interests in the United States had set their sights on obtaining clear title to Oregon Country. Settlers were drawn by tales of its fertile soil and mild climate. By the early 1840s, the famous Oregon Trail had already been etched into the American landscape by wagon trains heading for the Willamette Valley. One of Oregon Country's biggest boosters was Reverend Marcus Whitman, a Methodist missionary who had established a mission to convert to Christianity the indigenous people of the region. Whitman had been instrumental in showing that women and children could make the arduous overland trek by wagon. Less altruistic was the interest that shippers had in the region. The Pacific Northwest had deep ports vital to the extension of the China trade as well as the whaling industry. Thus, secure title to Oregon Country would advance Americans' goal of populating and using the resources of the continent as stressed in the ideology of Manifest Destiny. Polk, the Democratic candidate, promised not to settle for less than full title to the region clear to the fifty-fourth parallel. Polk also promised to annex Texas, giving Southern expansionists a reason to support him. Alluding to claims that Texas had been given away to Spain by John Quincy Adams in 1819, Polk campaigned for the "reannexation of Texas." This notion carried with it the idea of reattachment of a lost part rather than addition of something new.

The future course of history rested on the outcome of the election of 1844. Clay's election would maintain the status quo. Polk's election, conversely, would be a victory for expansionists, North and South, and would signal the beginning of a new era. Americans went to the polls on December 4, 1844, to cast their votes. Polk garnered a majority of the popular vote, winning 1,337,243 to Clay's 1,299,068. The Whig candidate still had a chance if he could carry the electoral college, but he came up short by seven votes when the electors met to cast their ballots. President Polk stood ready to make good on his promises.

Action on Texas, however, was under way even before Polk assumed office. John Tyler had moved ahead with plans to resubmit the Texas question to the U.S. Congress, this time asking both houses to decide the issue. A joint resolution from the House and Senate required less than the two-thirds majority needed by the Senate alone to ratify a treaty. Taking up the measure shortly after the start of the new year, the U.S. Congress extended an offer to Texas to join the Union. The bill would allow Texas to enter to the Union with all the rights and privileges accorded a full state, meaning that Texas could forgo the usual transition period spent as a territory. Moreover, Texas could keep its public lands, turning over only its military installations to the United States. On February 27 the Senate approved the resolution by two votes, twenty-seven for and twenty-five against. The margin was wider when the House voted the following day, 135 for and 76 against. The slave states by themselves had lacked the votes needed to bring Texas into the Union. Democratic support in New York, Pennsylvania, and Ohio had made Texas's statehood possible.

News of the successful passage of the joint resolution was received joyfully by most Texans. Still, some remained vehemently opposed to the Union, as in the case of one Mier prisoner, who warned,

"Part not so freely with that which has cost you your best citizens, at the Alamo, Goliad, and San Jacinto. Remain a nation of yourselves, or Nobly Perish."[13] But Texans had pursued statehood for nearly ten years. The United States was now asking twice-rejected Texas to consummate the union of the two republics. A special session of the Texas Congress met on June 23, 1845, to approve the measure. Texas President Anson Jones, Houston's successor, convened a special convention on July 4 to consider and accept the terms offered in the joint resolution. Jones then scheduled a plebiscite for October 13, in which citizens of the Republic of Texas could voice their opinions on the pending union. To no one's surprise, the vote reaffirmed their desire for statehood. On December 29, 1845, Polk signed into law the joint resolution that admitted Texas into the Union as the twenty-eighth state. In accepting statehood, Texas had rejected continued existence as an independent nation recognized by Mexico under a British-backed plan.

On February 19, 1846, dignitaries gathered in Austin to witness ceremonies formalizing Texas's entrance into the Union. President Jones delivered a brief address, which read in part: "May a gracious Heaven smile upon this consummation of the wishes of the two Republics, now joined in one. 'May Union be perpetual, and may it be the means of conferencing benefits and blessings upon the people of all the States,' is my ardent prayer." He ended with the words: "The final act in this great drama is now performed. The Republic of Texas is no more."[14]

Henderson Yoakum, soldier and historian, also wished the union of Texas and the United States well in his 1846 history of Texas. Writing of annexation, he said: "Here our labors end. Texas came into the Union for the love she bore it. While it prospers, Texas will prosper: their wars, their hopes, and their glory, are henceforth the same."[15]

NOTES

1. *Ross's Concession, January 29, 1833*. Daughters of the Republic of Texas Library, San Antonio, Texas.

2. Richard V. Francaviglia and Douglas W. Richmond, eds., *Dueling Eagles: Reinterpreting the U.S.–Mexican War, 1846–1848* (Fort Worth: Texas Christian University Press), 92.

3. Eba Anderson Lawton, ed., *An Artillery Officer in the Mexican War,*

1846–7: Letters of Robert Anderson (1911; Freeport, NY: Books for Libraries Press, 1971), 160.

4. Mattie Austin Hatcher, trans., "Joaquin de Arredondo's Report of the Battle of the Medina, August 18, 1813," *Quarterly of the Texas State Historical Association* (January 1908), 220–236. For an in-depth study of the Gutiérrez-Magee expedition, see Ted Schwarz, *Forgotten Battlefield of the First Texas Revolution: The Battle of the Medina, August 18, 1813* (Austin: Eakin Press, 1985).

5. Ernest Wallace, David M. Vigness, and George B. Ward, eds., *Documents of Texas History*, 2d ed. (Austin: State House Press, 1994), 48.

6. H. P. N. Gammel, *Laws of Texas, 1822–1897* (Austin: Gammel Book Company, 1898), 1:132.

7. Ibid., 1:424.

8. Ibid., 1:189.

9. Ibid., 1:213.

10. Alleine Howren, "Cause and Origins of the Decree of April 6, 1830," *Quarterly of the Texas State Historical Association* (April 1913), 416.

11. Gammel, *Laws of Texas*, 1:1069–1085.

12. Wallace, Vigness, and Ward, eds., *Documents of Texas History*, 143–144.

13. Joseph D. McCutchan, *Mier Expedition Diary: A Texan Prisoner's Account*, edited by Joseph Milton Nance (Austin: University of Texas Press, 1978), 116.

14. Herbert Pickens Gambell, *Anson Jones: The Last President of Texas*, 2d ed. (1948; Austin: University of Texas Press, 1964), 419.

15. H. Yoakum, *History of Texas* (New York: Redfield, 1856), 2:444.

CHAPTER FOUR

ACT TWO
To the Halls of the Montezumas

Oh, war now blows her ringing blast,
And fighting times have come at last,
Freedom buckle on the sword,
To crush the Mexican vile horde,
    Then march true freemen, march,
    Come march true freemen, march,
    March day and night, and boldly fight,
    For freedom and for Texas.
        Heigh ho united go,
        To crush the Dons of Mexico.
—"The Battle Call"
The National Songster (ca. 1848)

AMERICANS HAD BEEN at odds with Mexico over Texas since the filibustering days of the Gutiérrez-Magee expedition. The period of colonization initiated by the granting of an *empresario* contract to Moses Austin seemed to indicate that there may have been a peaceful way to acquire Texas. Such observers as Mier y Terán and Juan Almonte clearly saw that Texas, although nominally still part of Mexico, was rapidly becoming an extension of the United States through a preponderance of immigrants who were destined to impose their customs and cultures on the region. Friction between the colonists and Mexican officials turned into hostility that spawned an independence movement that bore fruit in 1836. Citizens of the Republic of Texas lived under the constant threat of invasion by Mexico and were fortunate that internal and external distractions prevented that country from focusing its full attention on reconquest. With Texas's statehood finally accomplished, many people in the United States, Mexico, and Texas believed that the real conflict between the United States and Mexico was about to begin.

    The United States had prepared for the possibility of hostilities with Mexico over Texas's annexation. In April 1844, President John Tyler ordered a buildup of U.S. troops at Fort Jesup, located just east of the Texas-Louisiana border. The action was taken to alleviate Texan concerns that passage of the pending annexation treaty would result in renewed hostilities with Mexico, and it recognized the fact that Texas's own attempts at building a regular army and navy had been unsuccessful. Although the Senate failed to ratify the treaty, the Army of Observation did not disperse but remained at Fort Jesup while the annexation drama continued to be played out in Washington. However, the passage of the joint resolution that extended statehood to Texas initiated a change in the situation. In June 1845, President James K. Polk ordered Brigadier General Zachary Taylor, commander of the Army of Observation, to advance into Texas. As acceptance of the statehood offer at the annexation convention in Austin on July 4, 1845, was considered to be almost certain, concerns over hostilities with Mexico again surfaced.

    Taylor and his expeditionary force (renamed the Army of Occupation once it landed on Texas soil) spent the next six months camped near the mouth of the Nueces River. Located on the north bank of the river, the encampment proved an economic boon to the small village of Corpus Christi. Merchants and vendors of all sorts flocked to the vicinity to sell their wares to the 3,400 U.S. troops camped along the beach. Soon a newspaper sprang up to supply the soldiers with the latest news. A troupe of actors came from New Orleans to perform at a theater opened by enterprising army officers who thought their men and comrades would pay to see professionally staged plays. Other types of entertainment abounded, too, involving gambling, liquor, and women. Although the cold, wet winter and blowing sand proved bothersome, many men enjoyed the opportunity to fish, hunt, and explore the surrounding area. The camp at Corpus Christi turned out to be a sportsman's paradise, and many in the Army of Occupation retained fond memories of it.

    Taylor used his stay at Corpus Christi to train his army, a fact that worked to his nation's advantage once fighting between the United States and Mexico occurred. This was the largest gathering of U.S. troops since the War of 1812, and many of the junior officers had never seen entire regiments and brigades together, let alone commanded soldiers in battle. The army's senior officers had been young men in 1812, but now most were incapacitated by age and unable to undergo the rigors of a military campaign. Luckily for the army, many of the midlevel and low-level officers had been trained at the U.S. Military Academy at West Point, giving Taylor a dedicated leadership cadre that took intense pride in its profession. Many of these young officers believed that the approaching battles would allow them to prove themselves both professionally and personally. By the time General Taylor left Corpus Christi in March 1846 he commanded a cocky, well-trained army. "We looked with confidence for a fight," later recalled Lieutenant James Longstreet, destined one day to be a Confederate general.[1]

Historians have often pointed out that the Civil War armies of 1861–1865 benefited from experience gained by such men as Ulysses S. Grant, Robert E. Lee, George Gordon Meade, James Longstreet, and a host of other young officers for whom the battles in Mexico provided a first chance to lead men under fire. Meade, the future Union victor of Gettysburg, recalled that more than thirty of his comrades who served in Mexico rose to the rank of general during the Civil War. Counting only West Pointers, Meade failed to mention the nearly 350 volunteers who later would reach that same rank as commanders of Southern and Northern troops. Thus, the approaching conflict offered opportunities to learn the art of war to those who cared to study.

Taylor's move south had been ordered by Polk. In November 1845 the president had sent Louisiana Congressman John Slidell to Mexico on a diplomatic mission, with instructions to negotiate a treaty to readjust the border between that country and the United States. Wrangling over Slidell's credentials prevented Polk's agent from presenting his proposal to Mexican officials. Frustrated by Mexico's failure to respond favorably to Slidell's offer to settle the Texas issue and other matters regarding territorial concerns, the president ordered Taylor to take up a new position on the Rio Grande. The Army of Occupation marched through the disputed Nueces strip unopposed and on March 28 halted across the river from Matamoros. Taylor established a depot near the mouth of the Rio Grande at Point Isabel, naming the post Fort Polk. He immediately began construction of a large earthen fortification, dubbed Fort

Texas, directly across from Matamoros and under the guns of Mexican soldiers, who watched in anger and dismay. There could be no doubt on the part of Mexican officials that they truly were facing an army intent not only on occupying but also on claiming the soil along the north bank of the Rio Grande.

Much attention has been paid by contemporary and modern writers to the disputed territory that lay between the Rio Grande and the Nueces River. The main contention has been that Mexico was willing to accept annexation if it could keep this 100-mile-wide strip of land that had historically been part of the Mexican states of Tamaulipas, Coahuila, and Chihuahua. But American expansionists had claimed Texas as a legitimate part of the United States clear back to the Louisiana Purchase. The Adams-Onís Treaty, which alienated the United States claim to Texas, failed to convince them that Texas was lost. In the wake of the Mexican defeat at the Battle of San Jacinto, officials of the new Texas government established a precedent for designating the Rio Grande as the border of the new republic by insisting in the Treaty of Velasco that the area north of the river be free of any Mexican troops. In December of that same year the Republic of Texas Congress officially adopted the Rio Grande as its southern and western boundary. Even though Mexico had been able to defend its claim to New Mexico and had temporarily reoccupied such towns as San Antonio and Goliad in 1842, in private circles many Mexicans admitted that Texas, including the disputed territory, was lost.

Though many Mexican officials believed that war with their northern neighbor would be catastrophic, talk of peacefully relinquishing territory seemed traitorous to most Mexicans. Thus, Mexican politicians assumed a belligerent stance and blasted the United States for its action. After years of promising to drive the Americans from Texas, how could they publicly acknowledge this latest development? The issue of the disputed territory really made little difference, as events of the past forty years had placed Mexico and the United States on the path to war.

Internal political dissension hampered the Mexican government's response to Taylor's landing at Corpus Christi and his subsequent advance to the Rio Grande. Opponents of President José Joaquín de Herrera, who accused him of being willing to accept Texas's permanent separation from Mexico, orchestrated one of the nation's all-too-familiar coups in order to replace him. On January 1, 1846, General Mariano Paredes y Arrillaga took over as president, vowing to protect Mexico's honor. Ironically, the general had been ordered by Herrera to reinforce the border, but instead he had used the troops at his command to overthrow his chief in a proposed monarchist plot. The task of opposing Taylor fell to General Pedro de Ampudia, a veteran of the battles of the Alamo and Mier. Because the appointed leader was unpopular with the people of Matamoros, Ampudia's detractors lobbied President Paredes for a more acceptable commander. He complied by sending General Mariano Arista, another veteran of the campaigns against the Texans, to thwart the advance of Taylor and to repel the perceived invasion of Mexican territory.

Taylor's occupation of the north bank of the Rio Grande could not go unopposed. The first to strike were Mexican rancheros (ranchers) who lived along both sides of the river around Matamoros. On April 10 a party of rancheros killed Colonel Trueman Cross, a senior U.S. officer who had wandered alone some distance from camp. When he failed to return, Taylor suspected foul play, but a quick search of the surrounding area revealed no clues. A small party of soldiers commanded by Lieutenant Theodoric Porter ventured out to look for Cross and was ambushed by rancheros. Several of the searchers, including Lieutenant Porter, were killed. Around this time, rancheros also attacked the camp of a detachment of Texas Rangers, again besting the Americans. Although small affairs by themselves, together these incidents convinced Taylor that they were only the prelude to something much bigger.

Indeed, something bigger was about to happen. Ampudia had planned to cross his troops to the north side of the river in order to turn Taylor's defenses but was ordered by his replacement, Arista, to delay any action until Arista arrived with reinforcements. The new commander decided on review that the plan proposed by Ampudia was sound. On April 24, a large column of Mexican troops commanded by Anastasio Torrejon crossed the river, thereby setting into motion a chain of events that would bring on the first major clash between the United States and Mexico. On the afternoon of April 25, 1846, a squadron of U.S. Dragoons sent to investigate rumors of the crossing stumbled into Torrejon's force near Carricitos, igniting a brief skirmish. Outnumbered and unable to escape, more than fifty dragoons surrendered, but not before fourteen of their men were lost in the brief engagement. Based on the latest events, Arista and his army had reason to be optimistic about their opportunity for success.

Taylor reacted quickly to the new development. He had two posts to protect from attack: his supply base at Point Isabel and Fort Texas across from Matamoros. His concern for Point Isabel was that Arista might overwhelm its garrison and thereby leave his army stranded in the interior with his line of communication broken. Placing Major Jacob Brown in charge of Fort Texas and its 500-man garrison, Taylor marched to the mouth of the Rio Grande with the rest of his army. Luckily for Taylor, Arista had not yet reached Point Isabel. On May 3, though, the Americans awoke to the sound of distant cannonfire that could only mean Fort Texas was under attack.

Taylor needed to know what was happening at Fort Texas. He accepted an offer from Samuel Hamilton Walker, commander of a small company of Texans attached to his army, to ride upriver and find out whether Major Brown could hold out until help arrived. A former Mier prisoner who had escaped from his prison quarters at Molino del Rey in Mexico City and walked to Tampico and freedom, Walker was known to be brave and daring. Traveling at night with only a few companions, the Texan slipped through the Mexican lines and inside Fort Texas. There he found the garrison in good spirits and in no mood to accede to Arista's demand that they surrender. Captain Walker carried the news back to Taylor, who determined to march to Fort Texas's aid. After making last-minute arrangements that included augmenting the army garrison at Point Isabel with sailors from U.S. ships anchored offshore, Taylor marched inland.

Arista had two objectives in attacking Fort Texas. First, if the fort could be carried quickly he would achieve an important strategic and psychological victory over Taylor. Not only would Taylor lose his foothold across from Matamoros, but the Mexicans could boast with pride that they had driven the invader from their doorstep. Even failing to capture Fort Texas, however, the attack would serve to draw Taylor away from his defenses at Point Isabel to ground of Arista's own choosing, a flat, grass-covered plain called Palo Alto (Tall Timber).

The two armies met on the afternoon of May 8, 1846. Taylor's scouts informed him that Arista had established a line of battle across the road leading from Point Isabel to Matamoros at Palo Alto. The Mexican force in front of him numbered 3,300. Taylor had fewer than 2,500 men. The general deployed his troops across the prairie from Arista, forming the wagons of his supply train in a square located to his rear. The battle was fought without much movement on either side. Musket balls tore through the opposing lines of soldiers. The novelty of combat for Taylor's untested army produced mixed emotions as the excitement of the fray clashed with the horror of seeing mangled bodies and hearing the cries of the wounded. A grass fire that had been started by burning wadding from a cannon halted the fighting until the wind swept the smoke away and the two lines could once more see each other. As nightfall approached, Arista pulled his bloodied army from the field and withdrew to a new position, leaving Taylor to declare victory.

While valor had not been lacking on either side, a technological advancement decided the battle. The U.S. Army had employed a type of artillery known as "flying artillery," which dramatically increased the mobility and firepower of that arm of service. Whereas on past North American battlefields cannon were drawn onto the battlefield by hand or draught animals and were left in one place, the U.S. Artillery at Palo Alto performed differently. Each gun had its own horse-drawn limber that contained a supply of ammunition. In addition, each member of the gun crew had his own mount. Thus, the unit could gallop anywhere on the battlefield that it was needed, unhook its guns, and unleash a storm of shot, shell, or canister against its surprised foe. Eager to prove the worth of "flying artillery" in its first test, the officers and men threw themselves into the battle without regard for safety. Their effort drove back several attempts by Arista's troops to advance that otherwise may have succeeded. Sadly for the U.S. artillerists, however, one of their casualties included Major Samuel Ringgold, the man who had convinced his superiors to adopt these tactics and had trained many of the officers and men in their use.

The following day, May 9, 1846, the battle was renewed, but this time flying artillery would be of less use to Taylor as he advanced toward Fort Texas. Arista had placed his troops in a dried streambed called Resaca de la Palma. Thick undergrowth provided cover for his soldiers and made it impossible for Taylor's light guns to maneuver. Arista hoped to recoup his misfortunes of the previous day by inflicting heavy casualties on Taylor's men as they attempted to penetrate the tangle of cactus and mesquite. Buoyed by their success, Taylor's troops pushed their way forward, but the limited visibility and mass of thorny vegetation made impossible the use of the linear tactics of the day. Instead Taylor's officers and men fought in small groups, sometimes not more than ten or twenty strong. Unable to see from which direction the enemy was advancing, Arista's line began to fall back. Panic spread through their ranks when U.S. Dragoons under Captain Charles May overran a Mexican battery guarding the road that snaked through the resaca and captured General Rómulo Díaz de la Vega. Afraid of being cut off, Arista's men headed to the river, seeking the safety of the opposite bank.

The U.S. garrison inside Fort Texas could hear the fighting getting closer. Soon a string of Mexican soldiers fled past, trying to make their way to Matamoros. The fort's troops could also see U.S. soldiers pursuing Arista's men out of the thicket. Desperate to escape, many of the fleeing Mexican soldiers threw themselves into the river, only to sink under the weight of their equipment or be shot as they attempted to swim across. The siege had been broken, and the garrison joined the jubilant celebration along with their rescuers. Sadly for the garrison, though, its commander—Major Jacob Brown—had been one of the two American fatalities produced by the siege. The earthwork, rechristened Fort Brown, would form the nucleus of the future town of Brownsville, Texas.

This first clash set the pattern for all other battles that would follow. The contestants were reminded that war, when stripped of honorable notions, was brutal business. Taylor reported that the fighting from May 3 through May 9 had cost him nearly fifty killed and more than 120 wounded. Arista reported sustaining 257 casualties of all types at Palo Alto and 388 more at Resaca de la Palma.

Several American officers recorded their impressions of battle. George Gordon Meade, then only a lieutenant of engineers, wrote his wife that he had been at Taylor's side for the entire battle and saw "some five horses and men" hit "right close" to him. He exclaimed, "I may justly say that I have had my *bepteme de feu* [baptism by fire]."[2] Another young lieutenant, Ulysses S. Grant, informed his fiancee that "although the balls were whizing thick and fast about me I did not feel a sensation of fear until nearly the close of the firing a [cannon] ball struck close by me killing once man instantly [and] nocked Capt. Page's under Jaw entirely off."[3] Even amid these horrific scenes, these men took note of acts of bravery. After four years of civil war, former Confederate general James Longstreet contended that "Many gallant, courageous deeds have since been witnessed, by none more interesting" than those seen at Resaca de la Palma.[4]

Hostilities between the United States and Mexico had begun. But was it really war? The question had actually been answered even before Taylor and Arista met on the field at Palo Alto. On Sunday, May 9, a courier arrived in Washington, DC, with a dispatch for President Polk describing the skirmish near Carricitos in which Torrejon had defeated and captured Captain Seth Thornton's command on the north bank of the Rio Grande. Polk, whose patience with Mexico had ended, was already drafting a war message to the U.S. Congress when he received this latest news. Claiming that "American blood had been shed on American soil," Polk finished his message, citing the attack as justification for war with Mexico.[5] In fact, according to Polk, the U.S. Congress did not need to declare war as it was clear that it already existed, pushed on the United States by Mexico's aggression against Taylor's command.

The House received Polk's war message on May 11, 1846; it passed the measure on to the Senate the following day. By an overwhelming majority the U.S. Congress voted to give the president the money and men he requested to prosecute the war. The regular army, too small to meet the emergency by itself, was to be augmented by a force of 50,000 state volunteers. Patriotism caused many U.S. Congressmen to accept Polk's version of the state of affairs at face value. The country echoed with cries of "On to Mexico" and "To the Halls of the Montezumas" as citizen-soldiers flocked to the colors.

Mexico was about to receive the brunt of pent-up frustration and hostility that had accumulated over the years. The emotional scars from such places as the Alamo, Goliad, Santa Fe, Béxar, Mier, and Perote were still raw and painful. David Crockett had been dead barely ten years when Taylor and Arista met in battle on the Rio Grande. These memories stirred men to action. In their eyes, Mexico must be made to pay for its crimes.

Americans were reminded of past deeds in popular songs such
as "Remember the Alamo," the words of which ran:

When on the wide spread battle plain,
The horseman's hand can scarce restrain,
His pampered steed that spurns the rein,
   Remember the Alamo.

When sounds the thrilling bugle blast,
And "charge" from rank to rank is past,
Then, as your sabre-strokes fall fast,
   Remember the Alamo.

Heed not the Spanish battle yell,
Let every stroke he gave them *tell*,
And let them fall as Crockett fell,
   Remember the Alamo.

For every wound and every thrust,
On pris'ners dealt by hands accurst,
A Mexican shall bite the dust,
   Remember the Alamo.

The cannon's peal shall ring their knell,
Each volley sound a passing bell,
Each cheer, Columbia's vengeance tell,
   Remember the Alamo.

For it, disdaining flight, they stand,
And try the issue hand to hand,
Woe to each Mexican brigand!
   Remember the Alamo.

Then boots and saddle! Draw the sword:
Unfurl your banner bright and broad,
And as ye smite the murderous horde,
   Remember the Alamo.[6]

Another popular song chided, "Think of the jails of Santa Fe, where
freemen in captivity, felt Mexico's foul tyranny," and vowed that
"our foes shall bow the knees, oh, to 'Yankee Doodle Dandy.'"[7] Yet
another cheered on "The Boys for Mexico" and boasted that priest-
ridden Mexico had "gold and silver images, plentiful and handy,"
implying that taking such religious paraphernalia was not stealing
but a laudable act that would reduce the power of the Catholic
Church, which held the Mexican nation in its grasp.[8] Calls for re-

venge and booty produced the army of volunteers that the nation needed finally to take the war to Mexico.

President Polk and his cabinet mapped out the strategy that would give the nation victory and at the same time redraw the national boundaries. Mexico would be attacked on several fronts at once. From the Rio Grande, Taylor would push on to Monterrey, the capital of the Mexican state of Nuevo León. Another column, called the Army of the West and commanded by General Stephen Watts Kearny, had two objectives: to seize both New Mexico and California. Once he reached the West Coast, Kearny could expect to receive aid from the U.S. Pacific Fleet that had been sent to the region in case war broke out. An offensive was also to be launched from New Mexico southward into the Mexican state of Chihuahua. This last force was supposed to be one-half of a pincer movement, with the other half leaving from San Antonio, Texas, under the command of General John E. Wool. Polk and his advisers believed that by seizing and occupying Mexico's northern tier of states, its leaders would be forced to sue for peace at terms favorable to the United States. The war and subsequent negotiations for peace, they imagined, would not take more than a year.

New Mexico was the first territory to fall to the United States. The Army of the West was quickly raised from Missouri Volunteers and organized around a small nucleus of Kearny's former regiment, the First U.S. Dragoons. Outfitted and mustered into service at Fort Leavenworth (Kansas), the Army of the West set off toward New Mexico in late June. The route was well known as they traveled along the road made famous by Missouri businessmen who, for years, had traversed the Santa Fe Trail. In late July the column reached the Arkansas River. Kearny stopped at Bent's Fort, a trading post established by brothers Charles and William Bent. The halt allowed Kearny's column to rest before moving on. The general sent an element ahead to scout the way through mountainous Raton Pass into New Mexico. These troops also had orders to overtake and capture an American trader traveling with the army who had made a dash to Santa Fe ahead of the military. Kearny had hoped to catch the New Mexicans unaware, and the departure of the trader threatened to spoil his plan.

The New Mexicans apparently already knew that Kearny's army was headed their way. The trail had been open all summer, and news of this sort traveled quickly. The governor of New Mexico and commander of its military was a person already known to the Americans—Manuel Armijo. Five years earlier, Governor Armijo had won acclaim in his country for capturing Texas President Mirabeau Buonaparte Lamar's Santa Fe Pioneers and sending the Texans off to captivity in Mexico City. While praised by his compatriots, Armijo became an archvillain in the United States, largely because of the popular writings of George W. Kendall, co-owner and editor of the *New Orleans Picayune*. This time, however, Armijo faced an army not already defeated by the environment and determined to succeed. Armijo unexpectedly allowed Kearny to pass through the mountains north of Santa Fe unopposed. The governor and his supporters then fled the city, leaving it to the Americans, who entered on August 18, 1846. As in the other towns through which Kearny had passed, the populace was informed by the general that New Mexico no longer belonged to Mexico but to the United States. Commented one newly created American citizen in broken English about this change of events, "*Armijo d—m rascal, gone to the d—l.*"[9]

Reminders of the Santa Fe Expedition greeted the Americans throughout New Mexico. Some residents sought to distance themselves from the infamous event, calling out "*bueno Americano*" whenever they encountered one of Kearny's men. Wrote one Missourian with an air of melancholy:

> While we marched down the valley of the great River of the North, feasting upon the melons of that sunny climate, it was impossible not to contrast our condition, as a triumphant army, with that of the wretched, and ill-fated Texan prisoners, who were captured near San Miguel, and conducted in chains and under guard down the same road, over the same ground, emaciated with hunger and ill-use, benumbed by the cold of winter, faint with sufferings, sinking under fatigues, and inhumanly butchered, by order of that monster of cruelty, Gen. Salezar, when they became too feeble to endure the hardships of the march. The remembrance of these outrages, practiced upon Texan and American citizens, so incensed the soldiers that they meditated wreaking vengeance upon the heads of unoffending Mexicans.[10]

The writer went on to posit that Christian forbearance on the part of his companions prevailed, keeping the innocent from suffering along with the guilty. Nevertheless, a preponderance of evidence indicates that many American soldiers did not share the spirit of forgiveness expressed in the Missourian's account.

As Kearny conquered New Mexico and the upper Rio Grande Valley, Taylor readied his army downstream for its advance into Nuevo León. He had spent the months following Palo Alto and Resaca de la Palma collecting troops and supplies for the campaign against Monterrey. So many state volunteers had arrived that he had to turn several thousand away. He occupied Matamoros on May 18 after the town had been evacuated by the Mexican Army. He sent detachments up the Rio Grande to seize the villages and towns along the south bank. He chose Camargo as his point of departure into the Mexican interior because steamboats carrying supplies could reach the town. Thus, Camargo became an important base in the American invasion and occupation of northern Mexico. On August 19, one day after Kearny's occupation of Santa Fe, Taylor's advanced guard left Camargo bound for Monterrey.

The route to Monterrey skirted the foothills of the eastern branch of Mexico's Sierra Madre. The route passed through the town of Mier, where on December 26, 1842, Ampudia accepted the surrender of more than 200 Texans who had crossed into Mexico in the wake of Woll's invasion. Curious American soldiers walked through the town's streets, examining the bullet-scarred buildings that lined the narrow passageways. They knew that the victor of Mier, Ampudia, had replaced Arista as commander after May's battles and awaited them at Monterrey behind that city's defenses.

The events of December 1842 clearly had not been forgotten. Governor J. Pinckney Henderson had secured a leave of absence from his office so he could personally lead his state's citizen-soldiers to war. At San Francisco, a small town south of Mier, one U.S. officer watched with interest several Texans who encountered a former captor: "Some of the Texans who were prisoners taken on the Mier expedition recognized a Mexican, . . . a man who had treated them with extreme cruelty in their passage through Mexico. . . . They beat him severely and probably would have killed him but for the imposition of some of our men."[11]

The soldiers took the Mexican to Taylor, who held him as a spy because he had been seen writing a letter, supposedly to officials in Monterrey. The officer described the constant back-and-forth retaliation he saw between the Texans and Mexicans as "tit for tat."[12]

By September 19, Taylor's army arrived on the outskirts of Monterrey, a place strikingly beautiful, the jagged mountains forming a natural backdrop. The general used the following day to survey Ampudia's defenses and to plan his attack. He divided his 6,640-man army into two wings and sent General William J. Worth to the western environs of the city with orders to seize Rinconada Pass, the pathway through the mountains to Saltillo. Control of the pass not only prevented help from reaching Ampudia but also blocked his escape. Once the pass was secure, Worth could assault the western defenses of the city and take possession of the heights that commanded Monterrey. Taylor established his headquarters and camp at Walnut Springs, a grove of trees several miles north of the city.

Worth's troops left their bivouac on the western edge of Monterrey soon after sunrise on the morning of September 21. His vanguard, composed of Texans commanded by Colonel John C. Hays, skirmished briefly with lancers formed across the road in line of battle. Texan rifles and Worth's light artillery soon drove the Mexicans back on their own defenses. Advancing, Worth's troops seized their first objective and then turned on the western fortifications. Two small redoubts topped Federation Hill, a low ridge that overlooked Monterrey from the southwest. Control of Federation Hill would greatly strengthen Worth's position. Eager for a fight, Worth's troops rushed up the hillside and drove the Mexican defenders from their posts. With the day barely begun, Worth had achieved a significant advantage over the enemy in his sector and at minor cost to his troops.

Things did not go as well for the Americans who attacked the eastern end of the city, though. Taylor had intended to support Worth's action by creating a diversion on the opposite side of Monterrey. It was a sound tactic as it would force Ampudia to split his forces in order to contend with both threats. Taylor erred, however, by becoming bogged down in a brutal slugging match with well-entrenched Mexican soldiers who occupied a series of small forts guarding the eastern approaches to the city. The first battalions sent in by Taylor ran into stiff resistance when they tried to enter the town. Determined not to be beaten by Ampudia, Taylor ordered in reinforcements, who fared little better at first. The problem for Taylor's men was created in part by the fact that the Mexican houses provided the defenders with ready-made fortresses. As at Béxar in

1835 the flat-topped roofs surrounded by low walls made excellent firing platforms from which to fire at anyone who ventured onto the street below. The thick adobe and stone walls provided protection from rifle and musket shot. Taylor's men quickly realized that the entire city was fortified. Even Taylor's vaunted flying artillery could do little in the confines of the narrow streets. The only bright spot of the day on the eastern side of Monterrey was the capture of two small forts, Tenería and El Diablo, giving Taylor a toehold from which the attack could be renewed the next day. That evening, Taylor's troops made their way back to Walnut Springs, leaving a small detachment to guard their hard-won possessions.

The night brought rain that made for a miserable time for all. Both sides used the darkness to recover their wounded. Bivouacked in the open, the soldiers of Taylor's army spent a cold, hungry, and sleepless night. Although provided with shelter, Ampudia's army had problems of its own as its officers quarreled among themselves, spreading discord down through the ranks and undermining their men's spirit.[13]

Worth used the weather to his advantage by planning an attack on Independence Hill, an even bigger prize than the one gained the day before. Separated from Federation Hill by the Santa Catarina River, Independence Hill held two Mexican positions: a small redoubt and an impressive structure known as the Bishop's Palace. Relying on Hays's Texans as well as U.S. regulars, Worth ordered the attackers to ascend the steep sides of the hill in the darkness. Just prior to dawn the defenders were surprised to find the enemy upon them. Quickly abandoning the small outworks, the Mexicans raced for the safety of the Bishop's Palace. Fast on their heels, though, were the Texans and regulars, who were able to enter the castle before the doors were bolted. With the Americans controlling the cannon of the slightly higher redoubt that overlooked their position, the defenders of the Bishop's Palace were faced with the choice of staying to receive Worth's fire, surrendering, or fleeing. Worth's men had accomplished another incredible feat. Although Taylor declined to renew the assault on the eastern side of the city, Ampudia and his soldiers were now within range of batteries manned by Worth's men on Independence Hill.

September 23 marked the third day of fighting at Monterrey. On the previous day only Worth was active; now Taylor resumed his push from the east while Worth's troops moved in simultaneously from the west. Throughout the day, Ampudia fell back toward the main plaza, begrudgingly giving up ground. The opponents battled from house to house, reminiscent of the fighting at Béxar in 1835. In fact, a number of Texans, veterans of the fight at Béxar, showed other Americans how to avoid the fire in the streets by breaking through walls, thereby advancing under cover. Moving house by house and block by block, the attackers made steady progress toward the main plaza. To their dismay, however, Taylor ordered all but a few detachments out of the city as darkness approached. Many of his soldiers thought victory was only moments away when the incomprehensible order came. Both sides prepared during the night for more fighting the next day.

However, instead of renewed fighting, September 24 brought an end to the battle. Ampudia had sent a delegation with a proposal to Taylor late the evening before. His aides explained that the cathedral on the main plaza near their chief's headquarters served as a makeshift magazine for ordnance supplies. A direct hit on the building, they warned, would cause a massive explosion that would kill many innocent civilians as well as inflict heavy casualties among Taylor's own soldiers. If allowed to leave with his troops and small arms, Ampudia would turn the city over to Taylor and withdraw below Saltillo while their respective governments could negotiate a peace.

To Taylor, engaged in a desperate struggle deep in Mexican territory and far from any possible support, an armistice seemed an acceptable end to the Battle of Monterrey. Each side appointed a delegation to work out the terms of the agreement. Acting for the Americans were General Worth, Colonel Jefferson Davis, and Texas's Governor J. Pinckney Henderson. Ampudia's representatives included J. M. Ortega, General Tomas Requena, and Manuel M. Llano. The terms of the armistice called for Ampudia to leave public property for the Americans, excluding the small arms in the hands of his soldiers and one six-gun battery. The Mexican troops were required to withdraw beyond a line formed by Rinconada Pass, Linares, and San Francisco de Pusos. On September 26 the Mexican Army's evacuation of Monterrey began, being completed two days later.

Regardless of how their commanding general felt about the armistice, many of Taylor's men were convinced that they had been cheated out of a real victory over the Mexicans. They wondered aloud why they had been ordered out of town on the night of September 23 when the contest seemed to be almost over. Some recalled the lenient terms granted General Cos following the Battle of Béxar. Paroled and allowed to march out with their small arms, Cos and his soldiers broke their promise to take no further part in the revolt by returning to Texas with Santa Anna. Left intact with its arms, would not Ampudia's army return someday in the not-too-distant future? To Taylor's detractors, the armistice spoiled what would otherwise have been a glorious victory. For some, his decision to accept such an arrangement drew into question his ability to command.

Even though Taylor had committed himself to eight weeks of inaction, movement against Mexico continued on other fronts. On September 23 advance elements of General Wool's Army of the Center left San Antonio bound for the Rio Grande. Composed predominantly of state volunteers, Wool's force had orders to march to Chihuahua and unite with a column of Kearny's Army of the West marching down from New Mexico. Wool's route crossed the Rio Grande at Presidio, where Santa Anna had crossed into Texas in 1836. He soon received news of the Battle of Monterrey and Taylor's armistice. Owing to this latest development, Wool halted his column at Monclova, the old federalist capital of Coahuila and Texas, in observance of the agreement.

Further to the west, the Army of the West continued its activities. Kearny established a territorial government for New Mexico, relying on assistance from lawyers serving in the ranks of his Missouri Volunteers. Not surprisingly, Americans made up a high percentage of the newly appointed governmental officials, included Charles Bent, who became the new governor. On September 25, Kearny departed for California with his regulars to complete the second phase of his mission. He left Colonel Alexander Doniphan behind with his regiment, the First Missouri Mounted Volunteers, to oversee the details regarding the continued occupation of New Mexico. Expecting reinforcements to arrive around the first of the new year, Doniphan prepared for his descent into Chihuahua and the planned rendezvous with Wool's Army of the Center. Leaving behind a small garrison at Santa Fe to assist civil officials, Doniphan marched southward toward the Rio Grande.

Mexican officials were determined to stop the American drive this time. Doniphan camped near the Rio Grande on Christmas Day

1846, unaware that he was about to be attacked. Many of his men were out gathering firewood when the advancing Mexican troops were spotted and had to rush back to the safety of the column's wagons to retrieve their arms. The Mexican commander, Lieutenant Colonel Antonio Ponce de León, asked for a parley, a request Doniphan rejected. León then ordered his troops to charge. The Missourians met the attack with a fusillade of musket and rifle balls, and the Mexicans quit the field, leaving behind forty killed or wounded. Doniphan could claim the Battle of Brazito as an inexpensive victory, with only seven wounded and none killed. With León defeated, Doniphan crossed the river and occupied El Paso on December 27, 1846.

Doniphan waited for reinforcements to arrive from Santa Fe before advancing on Chihuahua City. His force was further augmented by a large contingent of American traders whom he organized into their own battalion and added to his command. Leaving El Paso on February 8, 1847, the column traveled across nearly 250 miles of desert terrain in the following weeks. On February 28, fifteen miles short of his destination, Doniphan encountered yet another Mexican army blocking his path, as nearly 3,000 soldiers under General José A. Heredia occupied the high bluff opposite the Sacramento River. Even though his force numbered only about one-third of his opponent's, Doniphan decided to attack. Once more his small band proved victorious, breaking the Mexican lines and driving Heredia's soldiers from their breastworks. Mexican losses numbered 169 killed, 300 wounded, and 79 prisoners, as measured against four Missourians killed and eight more wounded. The victorious Doniphan entered Chihuahua City on March 2, 1847, without further opposition.

The question that Doniphan and his men asked themselves was what had become of Wool's Army of the Center? Cut off from any source of news, the Missourians had no idea how the war was progressing in other areas. They had been expecting word from Wool for weeks, but nothing had been heard. Isolated deep in Mexico, little could the Missourians know that other Americans then in the field had encountered difficulties that threatened to reverse the progress that had been made in California, New Mexico, and even Nuevo León and Coahuila.

Kearny, who had set out from Santa Fe in late September, learned from a chance encounter with Kit Carson that California had already fallen. The famed scout was on his way to Washington, DC, with official dispatches containing the news. In March 1846, Americans living in northern California had rallied around John C. Frémont, a U.S. officer leading what was supposed to be a scientific expedition exploring the Rocky Mountains and Pacific Coast. Frémont and the expatriates formed an alliance and pronounced themselves in revolt against Californian officials. Called the Bear Flag Revolt because the banner the group carried depicted a grizzly, the movement succeeded even though it had little support from the local residents. Later that spring the U.S. Navy arrived off the Californian coast to provide Frémont and the Bear Flaggers assistance. Commodore John D. Sloat, commander of the Pacific Squadron, landed U.S. sailors at the ports of Monterey and Yerba Buena (San Francisco), claiming the region for the United States. Frémont quickly abandoned the Bear Flag ploy and began referring to himself as the military commander of U.S. forces in California. Sloat's successor, Commodore Robert F. Stockton, continued to cooperate with Frémont as he and his volunteers moved down the coast. By early August, San Diego and Los Angeles were in U.S. hands and California appeared to be secure.

Learning of these developments from Carson and the dispatches he carried, Kearny ordered most of his troops back to Santa Fe while he continued on to California, taking Carson and only a small escort with him. The situation in California had changed, however, as the general was soon to learn. The Californios may not have liked taking direction from distant Mexico City, but the thought of being shut out of their own local government was unthinkable. Taking advantage of internal strife between their conquerors, the recently displaced officials, led by brothers Pío de Jesús and Andrés Pico, stirred their supporters into revolt, taking the Americans completely by surprise. The main towns were retaken, and Frémont was placed on the defensive.

Kearny was unprepared for this latest turn of events. The winter march across the mountains and deserts of New Mexico and Arizona had worn down his small, 100-man detachment. Food and water had been scarce for his men and their mounts, leaving both very weak. On December 6, 1846, Kearny's detachment encountered a band of lancers led by Andrés Pico near San Pasqual, California, and was badly cut up. The Californios killed twenty-one of Kearny's soldiers and wounded another seventeen, including the general. Without supplies and unable to travel, Kearny's command occupied a small hilltop while they waited for a relief party from the coast to come to their aide. The arrival of a naval detachment saved Kearny from several possible unpleasant scenarios: starvation, surrender, or outright annihilation.

The arrival of Kearny, even though bloodied and with only a handful of reinforcements, infused new life in his countrymen. Together with Stockton's sailors, Kearny's dragoons marched out of San Diego determined to crush the revolt. On January 8, 1847, the insurgents and Americans met and fought a battle at San Gabriel, a community near Los Angeles. The Americans may have taken pride that the date marked the thirty-second anniversary of Andrew Jackson's victory over the British at New Orleans. The Californios left the field in defeat but renewed the battle on January 9. Victorious at the Battle of Los Angeles, Kearny's and Stockton's men entered the town the next day and again raised the U.S. flag.

The Treaty of Cahuenga, signed on January 12, 1847, officially ended resistance to U.S. rule in California. Stockton had sent for Frémont, who had returned to northern California with his command, when the revolt in the south erupted. The young officer marched to his chief's aid but failed to arrive in time for the fighting around Los Angeles. He met the remnants of the insurgent army at Cahuenga Pass as it marched north. He accepted their offer to surrender, granting them generous terms. Although angered by Frémont's presumption that he had the authority to enter into such an important agreement, both Stockton and Kearny had little choice but to acknowledge the treaty.

California had not been the only U.S.-occupied territory to revolt. Kearny's and Doniphan's departure from New Mexico had left the newly installed government vulnerable. In December 1846 the occupation troops, under Colonel Sterling Price of Missouri, uncovered a plot involving the former alcalde (mayor) of Santa Fe and other former New Mexican officials. Some of the conspirators fled and others were punished, but the situation remained unsettled.

The real test of power came when the Pueblo Indians of Taos

rose up on the night of January 19, 1847, and murdered Governor Charles Bent and several other officials of the new government. The uprising spread rapidly, with attacks on the small garrisons at Turley's Mill and Mora. Price quickly reacted to the emergency, putting together a force of Missouri Volunteers, Santa Fe traders, and U.S. regulars that numbered approximately 350. He marched northward from his base at Santa Fe toward Taos. The winter weather and the mountainous terrain, both rugged, failed to slow his advance. On January 23, Price encountered and defeated a force of nearly 1,500 rebels who tried to block the narrow pass at Santa Cruz de la Cañada. Pushing northward, Price again encountered and routed the rebels near the town of Embudo in the narrow canyon through which the Rio Grande flows. The insurgents fell back to Taos, where they sought shelter in the thick-walled buildings that made up the pueblo. Adobe provided little defense against cannon when Price attacked the village on February 4. The insurgents surrendered the following day, and the Taos Revolt was over. The leaders of the uprising paid for their actions with their lives, either killed in the fighting or tried and executed in the days that followed Price's victory at Taos.

As incredible as it seemed, even Taylor's hold on northern Mexico had been threatened as 1846 drew to a close and the new year arrived. To Polk and his cabinet, the value of Taylor's victory at Monterrey was negated by the armistice he had signed with Ampudia. The president sent word to Taylor to break off the truce and resume offensive actions immediately. Polk, who had hoped that the war would be over by then, decided the situation demanded a new strategy as well as a new commander. He reluctantly turned to Major General Winfield Scott, commanding general of the army and a man whom he disliked personally. The revised strategy required Taylor to establish a defensive line in the area of Monterrey while Scott opened a new front by landing at Vera Cruz and then marching inland to Mexico City. Taylor would not only lose his position as the highest-ranking officer in Mexico, but most of his troops were slated to be reassigned to Scott.

Taylor had resumed his advance as instructed before learning of Scott's appointment. By mid-November, Worth's division had traversed Rinconada Pass, entering Saltillo on November 17 without resistance. Rumors began to circulate that a Mexican Army was on

its way to retake northern Mexico. When Worth asked Taylor for reinforcements, the general responded by diverting Wool to Saltillo,
thereby terminating his advance into Chihuahua and preventing the
rendezvous with Doniphan. Although no Mexican Army material-
ized, the threat to Taylor was real. The situation was made worse in
December and January when most of Taylor's veteran troops were
siphoned off to Tampico, where they were reorganized into Scott's
invasion force.

Polk and his supporters in the U.S. Congress realized that their
hope of a short war had been overly optimistic and that the armies
in the field would soon face critical shortages when the twelve-
month volunteers returned home. In November 1846 the War Department issue a second call for volunteers, relying on the unfilled
portion from the first mobilization bill. Even with this measure, it
would be well into the new year before these new levies reached the
front. In another move to strengthen the army, the U.S. Congress de-
bated a plan to create ten new regiments of regulars. Partisan wrangling prevented passage of the Ten Regiment Bill until February 11,
1847. Although they eventually produced results, these actions did
not provide any immediate help for Taylor.

Polk's administration had done more than just leave Taylor short
of troops; it unwittingly pitted him against Mexico's most famous
military chieftain, Antonio López de Santa Anna. The U.S. government had been approached in the summer of 1846 by a representative of the former leader, then exiled in Cuba. The ousted Mexican
president offered a deal: He would work to bring peace between the
two countries if allowed to pass through the U.S. naval blockade.
Polk and his advisers agreed and, in September 1846, Santa Anna
stepped off a British ship onto the dock at Vera Cruz. Home once
again, he abandoned his promise to Polk and threw himself into the
war effort. Given overall command of the army, he was formally
elected president on December 6, 1846. In a strange twist his vice
president was once again Valentín Gómez Farías, the radical liberal
who had served in Santa Anna's administration prior to the Texas
Revolution. Together the two men appealed to the various elements
of Mexican society—Santa Anna to the conservatives and Gómez
Farías to the liberals. Even though the church soon forced Gómez Farías's removal because of his policy of seizing its property to

finance the war, the pair was able to build an army that Santa Anna was about to launch against Taylor.

Rumors of Santa Anna's advance persisted. The U.S. commander at Saltillo after Worth's departure was William O. Butler, a general of volunteers from Kentucky. Butler decided to send a small scouting force toward San Luis Postosí to investigate the route that the Mexican Army would have to follow in its advance northward. The combined detachment of Arkansas and Kentucky Volunteers had orders to ride as far as Hacienda de Encarnación fifty miles away. The party reached its destination but decided to continue further. Encountering rain, the volunteers returned to Encarnación for the night. Wet, tired, and undisciplined, the detachment retired without posting adequate sentinels. They awoke on the morning of January 23 to find the hacienda surrounded by at least 3,000 lancers under General José Vicente Miñon. As the volunteers numbered fewer than 100, they surrendered when informed that they would be treated as prisoners of war. During their march into captivity, a former Texas Ranger named Daniel Drake Henrie escaped to tell their tale. The Texan had reason to take the risk, as his captors most likely would have killed him if they had realized Drake, a former Mier prisoner, had broken out of Perote Castle in the company of Thomas Jefferson Green less than four years earlier.

Taylor, still angry over Polk's order to abandon offensive operations, traveled to Saltillo to assess the situation for himself. Rumors that Santa Anna was on the way persisted. Taylor turned to Captain Ben McCulloch, commander of a Texas spy company, to bring him the proof he needed. McCulloch, who had been a neighbor of David Crockett back in Tennessee, would later be killed by Union forces at the Battle of Pea Ridge. Accompanied by only a few companions, he left Taylor's camp on February 20 and traveled to Encarnación. Reaching the hacienda at night, they observed thousands of soldiers huddled around campfires to keep warm. McCulloch wrapped himself in a blanket and descended on foot from the hills overlooking the Mexican camp. Walking from campfire to campfire, he learned that these were indeed Santa Anna's men and that the general was nearby. Rejoining the other Texans, he rode back to Taylor with the important news.

Taylor prepared for the impending battle. His army numbered

approximately 4,500, most of whom were volunteers from Arkansas, Illinois, Indiana, Mississippi, and Texas. Many of these men were from Wool's Army of the Center that had marched from San Antonio. Taylor's regular infantry, veterans of the battles on the Rio Grande and at Monterrey, had been appropriated by Scott for the upcoming landing at Vera Cruz. Taylor fortunately had been allowed to retain three batteries of his flying artillery as well as two companies of dragoons. Taylor personally oversaw preparation at Saltillo, where a small earthen fortification guarded the entrance to the city from the south. He had established his supply base at the Hacienda de Buena Vista, located several miles below the city. Two companies of Mississippians, a light field piece operated by U.S. regulars, and armed teamsters from the Quartermaster's Department stood ready to defend the post. Perhaps they were aware that this was the same hacienda at which Mexican federalists and Samuel Jordan's Texans had battled Rafael Vásquez's centralists in 1840.

Taylor left disposition of the troops to Wool, his second in command. The road from Saltillo to San Luis Postosí passed though a flat valley floor flanked on the east and west by high mountains. Arid and windswept, the terrain offered little comfort to travelers. The valley narrowed about seven miles south of Saltillo at a place called La Angostura (The Narrows). Wool chose this spot on which to establish his line of defense. Nature assisted him by providing an impenetrable maze of deep gullies west of the road; thus, he could concentrate his troops to the east. He placed several artillery pieces on the heights overlooking the road and extended the line of battle to the left using his volunteer infantry. He ordered the volunteer cavalry from Arkansas, Kentucky, and Texas to dismount and ascend the foothills to anchor the extreme left of his line. He also dispatched to that spot a small battalion composed of Indiana and Texas Volunteers armed and equipped as riflemen. Having prepared as best they could, Taylor, Wool, and their men settled down for the night, wondering what the morning would bring.

Santa Anna and his army arrived on the morning of February 22 with great fanfare. Ironically, he had passed this way in 1836 on his way to put down the rebellion in Texas. Santa Anna had left San Luis Postosí with more than 20,000 men this time, but desertions and the grueling march had reduced his effective force to around 15,000. Still, he had a 3-to-1 numerical advantage over his enemy. He halted his army within sight of Taylor but out of range of the American guns and reviewed his troops. Santa Anna dispatched a messenger to Taylor with a demand for his surrender that read:

> You are surrounded by twenty thousand men, and cannot, in any human probability, avoid suffering a rout, and being cut to pieces with your troops. But, as you deserve consideration and particular esteem, I wish to save you from a catastrophe, and for that purpose give you this notice, in order that you may surrender at discretion, under the assurance that you will be treated with the consideration belonging to the Mexican character. To this end you will be granted an hour's time to make up your mind, to commence from the moment when my flag of truce arrives in your camp.[14]

Taylor declined the offer and the battle commenced. One must wonder whether Taylor and his men recalled that the morrow marked the eleventh anniversary of the commencement of the siege of the Alamo, conducted by Santa Anna under the infamous Tornel Decree.

Taylor's critics had been correct when they predicted that he would meet Ampudia again on the battlefield: The defeated general and his troops had been attached to Santa Anna's new army. Santa Anna ordered Ampudia to drive the dismounted volunteers and riflemen from the foothills and turn the Americans' left flank. Throughout the afternoon and into the evening the troops positioned on the valley floor could gauge the progress of the fight by the muzzle flashes on the hillsides. Darkness brought an end to the fighting as a cold rain drenched both attackers and defenders.

Taylor returned to Saltillo that night to check once more on its defense. He took with him as escort two companies of U.S. Dragoons and the First Mississippi Rifle Regiment. The commander of the Mississippians was Colonel Jefferson Davis, Taylor's former son-in-law and future president of the Confederate States of America. The First Mississippi was the only volunteer unit (with the exception of McCulloch's spy company) that had been tested in battle, serving with distinction at Monterrey. Remaining in town that night, Taylor returned to the front lines the following morning to find that the battle had already resumed.

Santa Anna began the action with an attack straight up the road to Saltillo. The U.S. Artillery again proved its worth by effectively making the road too deadly to use. Not to be denied, Santa Anna struck Wool's left with columns of massed infantry. Wool's volunteers held at first but then gave way when the commander of the Second Indiana Infantry ordered his regiment to retreat. Only the desperate stand of Lieutenant John Paul Jones O'Brian and his section of regular artillery prevented a rout. This officer and his men manned their guns as the Mexican line rushed forward, hammering it with round after round of canister. Abandoning their guns only when the advancing line neared the muzzles of their pieces, O'Brian and his men bought Wool enough time to stabilize his line of battle.

Santa Anna continued to press Wool's left flank. The battered volunteers began to give way again, although without the confusion experienced earlier. Santa Anna's battalions actually succeeded in turning Wool's flank and made for Saltillo. It was at this point that Taylor returned to the battlefield. He ordered Davis to block the advance with his regiment. Augmented by members of the broken Second Indiana and the still-intact Third Indiana, Davis formed a V-shaped formation across the path of the charging lancers. Inexplicably, the lancers slowed to a halt, giving the Americans the opportunity to unleash a murderous crossfire. With the breakthrough contained, Taylor quickly reformed his line.

The elements of Santa Anna's army that had slipped by the American's left flank threatened Saltillo and the depot at Buena Vista. Fortunately for the men posted there, the attacks on their positions were not pressed home, and the Mexicans were easily driven off. Wool's line opened a devastating fire on the opposition forces as they retreated southward along the foot of the mountains. At that moment a party of Mexican officers approached Wool under a white flag. The general ordered a cease-fire and rode forward to met them. They informed him that they were responding to his request for a parley. Denying he had asked for such a meeting, he sent them back to their own lines. The Americans believed that the white flag had been a ruse to allow the Mexican troops to escape from their unpleasant predicament.

More desperate fighting lay ahead. The colonels of the First and Second Illinois and First Kentucky led their infantry regiments forward across the valley floor. One feature of the terrain was a series of deep ravines that cut through the otherwise flat surface. Wool denied ordering the advance of these troops that ended in disaster. Hidden from view in the deep ravines were several thousand Mexican troops preparing for another assault on Wool's line. The unsuspecting volunteers were descending into the ravines just as the Mexican line moved forward. Many were cut down. The survivors raced back up the valley, pursued by the Mexican infantry and lancers. Once more it was the artillery that saved the day for Taylor. Captain Braxton Bragg, one day destined to command the Confederate Army of Tennessee, unlimbered his battery's guns and began blasting the advancing line. His action led to one of the war's more memorable moments, summed up in Taylor's reported request that Bragg give the Mexicans "a little more grape." Davis's Mississippians and the Third Indiana also rushed to the scene and added their fire to Bragg's. It was more than Santa Anna's soldiers could stand, and they broke off the attack.

Neither side attempted to renew the action as evening approached. As on the previous night, Taylor returned to Saltillo to check his positions there. He had suffered more than 650 casualties. Among the dead were Colonel Archibald Yell, former governor of Arkansas and friend of Andrew Jackson, and Lieutenant Colonel Henry Clay Jr., son of the famous Kentucky statesman. One of the wounded was Jefferson Davis, his ankle shattered by a Mexican musket ball as he sat astride his horse issuing orders to his regiment. Wool, still at La Angostura, readjusted his thin line, readying it for more fighting in the morning.

The morning dawned quiet. Patrols reported that the Mexican Army had withdrawn southward during the night, leaving the battlefield to Taylor and his men. Although both sides claimed victory, the Americans had not been driven away. Taylor named the battle after the hacienda where his supplies were kept, Buena Vista. Mexican accounts carried a different name, La Angostura. Mexican losses were estimated at around 3,400 dead and wounded. Taylor's scouting parties encountered dead, wounded, and dying *soldados* along the road to San Luis Postosí. In the opinion of one Mexican soldier, the withdrawal had been ordered because Santa Anna "doubted the results of a new battle the next day, and taking into consideration that the Republic had no other army with which to oppose the invader, who had already another army forming in the East, SANTA-ANNA, feared that if in a new battle he were overthrown, the Americans would penetrate into the very heart of the country without encountering any resistance."[15]

Taylor had clung to northern Mexico but just barely. Santa

Anna's advance had been timed to support an outbreak of guerrilla activity behind Taylor's lines clear back to the Rio Grande. General José Urrea, the officer who had captured Fannin and his men near Goliad in 1836, now commanded several groups of irregular troops operating between Monterrey and Camargo. He captured Cerralvo and held the town for a month. Urrea also captured a U.S. Army supply train that consisted of 110 wagons and 300 pack mules. Allowing the train's military escort to march away unmolested, Urrea's men killed forty to fifty teamsters, tying many of them to their wagons and burning them alive. A relief party from Monterrey finally reopened the road.

Not all of Urrea's men escaped retribution. One of Doniphan's men passing through on his way home witnessed the execution of a Mexican who had participated in the attack on the wagon train. One of the murdered men had been a Texan, whose brother was in the crowd assembled to watch the execution. The grieving sibling paid one of the members of the firing squad $5.00 in gold to take his place and thus had his private revenge.[16]

It is easy to underestimate the threat that the United States faced in February 1847 in light of the eventual outcome of the war. A Mexican victory at Buena Vista and a successful guerrilla offensive in northern Mexico could quite possibly have ended Scott's campaign before it began. And without an invasion at Vera Cruz the history of the war may have been much different.

〜 Scott's amphibious landing at Vera Cruz was a masterpiece of military planning and execution. Not only his 10,000-man army but tons of food, ammunition, ordnance, and other matériel had to set ashore safely if the invasion was to have any chance at success. But General Winfield Scott, a 40-year veteran of the army, had the training, ingenuity, and determination to accomplish the task. It required planning down to the minutest detail, but Scott excelled in such matters. Not until World War II would the United States again undertake a landing of this scale on enemy shores.

Scott arrived in Mexico around New Year's Day 1847 ready to begin operations. He had hoped to meet with Taylor to explain his plan to him in person, but his defiant subordinate failed to make an appearance on the Rio Grande while Scott was there. With Taylor unavailable, Scott issued orders directly to Taylor's brigadiers and assumed command over their troops. Many of Taylor's regulars marched back to Point Isabel where transport ships awaited them. Taylor had already ordered General John A. Quitman's volunteer division to march from Monterrey to Ciudad Victoria in an effort to secure the state of Tamaulipas. These troops received orders to continue their advance to Tampico, a port city near the mouth of the Pánuco River that would serve as a collection point for troops participating in the new campaign. The city had been under U.S. control since November 1846, when Commodore David Conner's home fleet captured it without a fight. During January and February several thousand American troops camped on its outskirts, waiting for preparations for the descent on Vera Cruz to be finalized.

The landing required cooperation between the army and the navy. While in theory an army operation, Scott's strategy depended on the navy not only to transport his troops to Vera Cruz but to provide fire support with its shipboard batteries. Commodore Conner and Scott worked well together, without the friction or rivalry usually associated with joint operations. Conner suggested that the actual landing be made at Collado Beach, several miles south of the city. He explained that Antón Lizardo, his nearby supply base, already had facilities that could be used to support the landing. Additionally, Collado Beach was out of range of the guns of San Juan de Ulúa, which guarded the harbor and city. Built in the 1770s, the massive stone fort usually was called a castle and was considered by military experts of the day to be one of the strongest fortifications in the Western Hemisphere.

Scott had chosen Vera Cruz as his point of debarkation because of its strategic location. One of Mexico's busiest commercial centers, the city lay at the eastern end of the road leading to Mexico City. Vera Cruz had a long history as an entry point for invaders, stretching back to Cortés's conquest of Mexico in 1519. More recently the city had been occupied briefly by the French in the 1838 Pastry War, which catapulted Santa Anna back into power after the disastrous Texas campaign. Home to a cosmopolitan population that included several hundred foreign nationals who conducted business in the port, Vera Cruz was central Mexico's outlet to Europe and the rest of the world.

Scott expected the city to be heavily defended, as its importance deemed it should be. In fact, Mexican military leaders had advance

warning of Scott's intention, as his plan had been discussed in newspapers in the United States prior to his departure for Mexico, much
to his chagrin. Moreover, guerrillas had killed a courier sent by Scott
to Taylor and found a detailed copy of the plan on his body. But
Mexico's internal political struggles were at work behind the scene,
diverting attention away from the crisis posed by Scott's planned
invasion.

The latest controversy centered around Vice President Gómez
Farías. The vice president had issued a decree on January 11, 1847,
that would in effect seize $15 million in church property to be used
to finance the war effort. All but his most liberal supporters turned
against him. Mexico City's civic militias, composed of middle-class
citizens, provided the military muscle for Gómez Farías's opponents. A revolt erupted on February 27 after the vice president ordered three of the militia battalions to Vera Cruz. The transfer of
these troops not only would reinforce that city's defense, but Gómez
Farías would be free from the militia's interference in government
affairs. The units refused to leave and called for both the repeal of
the January 11 decree and the vice president's resignation. Arriving
back in Mexico City after his battle with Taylor near Saltillo, Santa
Anna removed Gómez Farías from office and revoked the obnoxious
decree in return for a $2 million "loan" from the church. The Mexi-
can Congress abolished the office of vice president and created that
of substitute president in its place. General Pedro María Anaya,
a moderate, became substitute president in the continued absence
of Santa Anna. It is interesting to note that Santa Anna later used
the Revolt of the Polkos, as the incident was called, to explain his
sudden departure from the battlefield at Buena Vista, claiming that
events in Mexico City demanded his immediate attention, making it
necessary for him to break off the engagement. An examination of
the war's chronology, however, reveals that the revolt occurred after
the battle.

The Mexican military chief at Vera Cruz was General Juan Morales, a veteran officer who had led one of the assault column on the
Alamo on March 6, 1836. His force included the 1,000-man garrison
at San Juan de Ulúa and another 3,000 men inside the walled city.
The defenders possessed some 400 cannon, but the reinforcements
intended to bolster Morales's command were caught up in the Revolt of the Polkos and did not arrive before Scott's landing.

Scott's campaign officially commenced on March 9, 1847, with the landing of 10,000 men on Collado Beach. Astonishingly, his troops met no opposition as they came ashore. General Morales chose instead to keep the defenders inside the city and did not venture out to contest the landing of Scott's surfboats or make any forays outside the walls to threaten the Americans in the days to come. Scott began encircling Vera Cruz, at intervals building batteries from which to bombard the city. Running short of siege artillery, Scott allowed the U.S. Navy to bring ashore guns from aboard its warships for use against Morales. On March 21, with Vera Cruz surrounded, Scott sent a message to Morales announcing he would soon open fire on the city but that he would first allow all noncombatants to leave. Morales refused and the bombardment from the U.S. shore batteries and warships commenced the next day. Once the city and its inhabitants began to suffer the effects of the heavy shot and shell, the defenders asked for a truce to allow civilians to leave, but this time it was Scott who refused, knowing that their suffering would force a quicker end to the battle. General Morales resigned and was replaced by General Juan Landero, who surrendered the city and castle to Scott. The defenders marched out of Vera Cruz on March 28, turning the city and castle over to the Americans.

Scott had a beachhead for the invasion but had to move quickly to solidify his gains. The tropical coast was notorious for diseases, especially *el vómito negro* (yellow fever; literally, the black vomit): Troops had to march inland to the highlands before the return of the deadly hot season turned the city into a pestilence-ridden port. Scott had another reason to act quickly: A significant portion of his army was composed of 12-month volunteers whose enlistments were about to expire. The campaign must be pressed forward with speed, or he would be left with too few troops to achieve his objective.

On April 8, nearly a month to the day after the landing at Vera Cruz, the first elements of Scott's army marched inland. The tropical climate became more temperate as the troops steadily tread the steep highway leading into Mexico's interior. By April 11, Brigadier General David E. Twiggs's division had reached Plan del Río, where high cliffs formed the leading edge of Mexico's central plateau. An inconclusive skirmish demonstrated to the Americans that the pass was defended by a large number of troops who intended to block Scott's advance. Although the arrival of another division increased the Americans' strength, the U.S. commander on the spot, Major General Robert Patterson, decided to wait for Scott to catch up with the rest of his army before attacking.

Santa Anna would command the Mexican defenders at the Battle of Cerro Gordo. Returning to the capital after his encounter with Taylor at Buena Vista, he had assembled another army from the survivors of his advance on Saltillo, supplemented by fresh units raised to contest the invasion. His troops occupied the tops of three promontories on a line east to west—La Atalaya, El Telégrafo, and Cerro Gordo. Thirty-two pieces of artillery commanded the countryside from these hilltop fortresses. Santa Anna's position, guarded by nearly 12,000 soldiers, seemed impregnable.

Scott arrived on the scene and sent his military engineers to examine the terrain and find a way around Santa Anna's defenses. Based on the engineers' reports, he planned his assault for April 18. The action began earlier than he intended, however, when on April 17 the Mexicans fired on Twiggs, who in turn ordered Colonel William S. Harney to carry La Atalaya by force. The hilltop, which proved not to be as heavily defended as believed, was captured. During the night, one of Scott's engineers, Captain Robert E. Lee, oversaw the emplacement of two cannon atop La Atalaya that were hauled up the steep hillside by hundreds of infantrymen detailed to pull the drag ropes. At dawn, cannon fire from the hilltop began to rain down on the Mexican positions to the west. Harney's men charged El Telégrafo and carried its works. An attack by Major General Gideon Pillow's volunteer division against the Mexican right flank failed, but Twiggs's troops were able to turn Santa Anna's left and seize the road to Jalapa. The Mexican defenders, who were in danger of being cut off by the rapid movement, abandoned their works and retreated westward. Mexican losses included some 1,000 killed and wounded and another 3,000 captured. One of the prisoners was General Rómulo Díaz de la Vega, who had also been captured by the Americans at Resaca de la Palma. So suddenly did the Mexican line give way that Santa Anna narrowly escaped from the battlefield, leaving behind his carriage containing his papers, camp equipment, a cork leg, and a large amount of silver bullion for the Americans to plunder.

Scott ordered General William J. Worth, his one-time protégé and the hero of Monterrey, forward after the retreating army. Worth entered Jalapa on April 19, but Santa Anna and his troops had already dispersed, using roads known only to the local inhabitants of the region. Scott's army remained at Jalapa for nearly a month before advancing to Puebla in mid-May. While at Jalapa, the general dismissed the twelve-month volunteers who had accompanied him on his campaign thus far. Their departure depleted his ranks and left him in desperate need of reinforcements to mount his final push on the Mexican capital.

Scott's army passed by Perote Castle on its march to Puebla, a sight that inspired awe owing to its massive size and a sense of foreboding because of its dark past. Wrote one volunteer of the structure, "The Castle possesses a melancholy interest to our army. It was here that the [Mier] prisoners after having been marched in triumph over the greater part of Mexico were confined."[17] He was erroneously shown the spot "from which Capt. [Samuel H.] Walker and part of his companions escaped."[18] Although Thomas Jefferson Green had escaped from Perote, Walker had escaped from Molino del Rey. The recall of dramatic episodes involving the Texans caused the writer to contemplate the reason that Walker and his men usually took no prisoners: "when we consider the sufferings to which these men were exposed, abused in the grossest manner, a number of their party murdered while prisoners in cold blood, the feeling of retaliation which influences the survivors is in a great degree palliated and cannot be violently condemned."[19] Walker, then with the army in the capacity of the captain of Company C, U.S. Mounted Rifles, remained behind with his unit to help guard the stretch of road from Jalapa to Perote when the majority of Scott's army marched on to Puebla.

Puebla provided a pleasant respite for Scott's army. His troops were quartered in many of the city's public spaces, including the Plaza de Toros. Scott used his time well, ordering frequent drills to hone his troops' skills. The additional levy of volunteers "for the war" and new regular regiments began to arrive at Puebla in July. Scott carefully incorporated them into his reorganized army, continuing training for all his troops, old and new alike. When not drilling, the soldiers could roam the city at will and take in its sights. Many visited the ancient pyramid at nearby Cholula. By mid-August, Scott pronounced the army sufficiently prepared to undertake its biggest challenge yet, the assault on Mexico City.

Scott's vanguard reached the outskirts of the Mexican capital within a week of leaving Puebla. Before them lay the ancient capital of the Aztecs, stretched out on the floor of a great prehistoric lake-bed surrounded by snow-capped volcanoes. The Spanish conquistador Cortés found that the Aztecs had built their city on islands composed of floating masses of vegetation. Causeways connected the islands, making possible foot travel to and from the Aztec capital. Although much of the lake had been filled in over the subsequent 300 years, canals and marshes were still prominent features of the terrain. Causeways stretched out from the city like the spokes of a wheel, offering the attackers an inviting path to their prize. But this breathtaking landscape posed an obstacle as serious as the Mexican Army that defended Mexico City.

Santa Anna hoped that the invaders would take the most direct route into the city, a route guarded by a high hill named El Peñon where the Mexican commander had stationed 7,000 soldiers of General Gabriel Valencia's veteran Army of the North. Scott almost always chose maneuver over battle and relied on his engineers to find a way around Lake Chalco and Lake Xochimilco in order to move his army to the south and west, thereby sidestepping the Mexican fortifications. At the west end of Lake Xochimilco, however, Scott found his path blocked by a seemingly impenetrable expanse of volcanic rock, the remnants of an ancient lava field. He again turned to his engineers and ordered them to find a way through the maze of dark, jagged basalt. Returning from their mission, Captain Robert E. Lee and Lieutenant P. G. T. Beauregard informed Scott that they had located a small footpath that could be widened to allow artillery to pass. On August 19, Scott sent two divisions through the lava field to attack Mexican positions on the other side. Detected while still in the *pedregal* (lava field), these troops encountered stiff opposition that ended only when night fell. Despite the rough, uneven ground and a steady rain, Scott sent more troops into the lava field that night with orders to resume the battle at dawn. Lee, the future commander of the Army of Northern Virginia, was their guide.

On the morning of August 20 the Mexican troops defending the villages of San Antonio and Contreras awoke to find that they had been outflanked during the night and that Scott's men were behind them. Many surrendered once they determined that the situation was hopeless. With the road to the capital open, the Americans rushed northward. Blocking their path to Mexico City was the fortified convent of Churubusco. The defenders of Churubusco put up a much more stubborn resistance than Scott's men were used to encountering. Inside the convent were local national guardsmen who were fighting to keep the Americans out of their homes. Also inside was the San Patricio Battalion, composed of deserters from the U.S. Army. Both groups had good reasons to fight hard, but by afternoon the convent and a small fort guarding the crossing over the Churubusco River had fallen. Santa Anna's defenses had crumbled, and Mexico City was Scott's for the taking. Although many U.S. officers later received citations recognizing their participation in the battle, one who received special notice was Lieutenant Thomas J. Jackson, who would later be known by the name "Stonewall."

Scott chose not to enter the city after his victories at San Antonio, Contreras, and Churubusco. His troops were exhausted and disorganized. He wanted to maintain strict control over his army and believed that if he allowed his troops to enter the capital in their present excited state, they might sack the city. He also had a proposal from Santa Anna for an armistice. Scott knew that each battle, even a victory, whittled down the size of his small army. The fighting for the capital had so far cost him 139 dead and 1,876 wounded. The battles had cost Santa Anna approximately 3,250 killed and wounded and another 2,627 taken prisoner. A chance to negotiate an end to hostilities appealed to Scott, who therefore accepted the offer to avoid further bloodshed on both sides.

Like the armistices at Béxar in 1836 and Monterrey the year before, this agreement would be controversial. Many of Scott's men, in light of subsequent bloody fighting, believed that he had made a mistake in not following up the battles of August 20 by seizing the capital when the opportunity arose. His critics claimed that Scott had been duped by Santa Anna, who reportedly used the break in fighting to rebuild his defenses, contrary to the terms of the armistice. Moreover, teamsters and their escort, who were sent into the city to obtain supplies per agreement with Santa Anna, were attacked, providing both insult and injury to the Americans. Deciding that the negotiations taking place during the armistice would not yield the desired results, Scott gave Santa Anna notice on September 7 that the armistice was over and hostilities were about to resume.

During the armistice a story spread that the defenders were using an old mill, Molino del Rey, as a foundry at which they were casting cannon to replace those lost in the earlier battles to defend the city. The mill also had served as a prison for some of the Mier prisoners, including Samuel H. Walker. The mill complex was located two miles southwest of the city. Scott had moved his main force to this sector, establishing his camp at Tacubaya, a suburb that usually served as home to Santa Anna when he was performing the official duties of Mexico's president. North of Tacubaya lay the imposing castle of Chapultepec, once the residence of Spanish royalty and now home to the Colegio Militar, the Mexican equivalent of West Point. The castle loomed over the landscape, covering the surrounding area with its guns. An attack on Molino del Rey would have to stay clear of Chapultepec.

The assault on Molino del Rey took place early on the morning of September 8. Scott placed his most experienced lieutenant, General William J. Worth, in command of the operation that was supposed to clear out the defenders and destroy the foundry. Worth attacked with 3,400 men but quickly encountered serious trouble. Seven regiments of Mexican regulars and national guardsmen occupied the complex, supported by several pieces of artillery. As at Béxar and Monterrey, the Mexicans used the flat roofs of the mill complex to their advantage, firing from the protected parapets at the soldiers down below. Worth's casualties mounted, making defeat a likely outcome. Recovering from their initial setback, his men finally forced the defenders from their positions, who retired under the protection of Chapultepec's guns. The fighting at Molino del Rey proved to be the most costly for the Americans during the war. Worth's losses numbered nearly 800, a startling 23 percent of his division. Although Mexican losses numbered more than twice Worth's, Scott's army took little pleasure in the victory. No foundry existed at the mill, rendering the costly attack pointless.

In the wake of the bloody action at Molino del Rey, Scott reviewed his plan of operations with his senior officers and engineers. Most were in favor of an assault on the city's southern defenses because it was the most direct route, but Scott again opted for a flanking maneuver. He planned to leave a diversionary force to lock Santa Anna in his position at the southern approach, while directing his main columns down the western causeways to San Cosme and Belén Gates. His strategy meant that Chapultepec must be carried to clear the way for the assault.

Preparations for the attack commenced on September 12. General John Anthony Quitman's division mastered southeast of Chapultepec to draw Santa Anna's attention away from the movement of other units to the west. Santa Anna, convinced that the main attack on the city would come from the south, failed to realize what was happening, even when Scott's artillery unleashed a lengthy barrage on Chapultepec Castle on the morning of September 13. Once the firing ended, both Pillow's and Quitman's divisions began their assaults on the castle, climbing the steep hillsides under a withering fire from the defenders. Santa Anna, who had held most of his troops closer the city awaiting an attack on the southern gates, had allotted only 800 troops under General Nicolás Bravo to defend this important post. Battling their way to the summit, Pillow's and Quitman's troops, reinforced by Worth, overcame resistance and occupied the castle. One of the last groups of defenders to be subdued was the cadets from the Colegio Militar, who refused to surrender. In a daring act that impressed those who witnessed it, Lieutenant George E. Pickett, who would later lend his name to one of the most famous military actions of the Civil War, grabbed the U.S. flag from his wounded friend, Lieutenant James Longstreet, and carried the red, white, and blue banner to the castle's top.

With Chapultepec secured the action shifted to other areas. Quitman's division attacked northeastward along the causeway leading to the Belén Gate, while Worth's division swung north and west toward San Cosme Gate. The Americans at first were confined to the dry ground of the causeway, where they were exposed to fire from fortified gates. The fighting devolved into small-unit action with groups of soldiers wading through the marshes adjacent to the roadways to reach cover on the edge of the city. As at Resaca de la Palma, the army's success rested largely on individual initiative. Lieutenant Ulysses S. Grant oversaw the placement of a small artillery piece in a church tower, an act rewarded by an honorary promotion to captain. Lieutenant Thomas J. Jackson won another honorary promotion, this time to major, for directing his artillery piece while exposed to the enemy's fire. By night the defenders had been driven from the gates, which were occupied by men of Worth's and Quitman's divisions. Scott ordered a halt to the attack, but darkness brought little rest to the Americans poised to enter the city.

Before sunrise on September 14, Quitman advanced toward the city's main plaza and occupied the National Palace. Surprisingly he met no formal opposition when he entered Mexico City. During the night, Santa Anna had held a council of war with his senior officers and city officials in which they determined that continued resistance would only increase the amount of suffering already experienced, making the city itself a battleground and thereby endangering innocent lives and property. The fighting on the thirteenth had already produced 3,000 dead, wounded, and prisoners, in addition to those already lost in the previous battles for the capital. Although Scott's casualties numbered around 850, he still commanded a force sufficient to take the city by force if necessary. A delegation from the city approached the general at Tacubaya shortly after midnight, offering to surrender the city to him. The usually diplomatic Scott informed them that he did not need to discuss terms with them because the city was already his.

The situation did not stay quiet for long. Santa Anna's retreating army had opened the prisons on its departure and released the city's convicts into the streets. Joining with other disruptive elements, they began to loot shops and throw stones at the Americans around the National Plaza. Sporadic gunfire also broke out as unseen gunmen fired on the occupation forces. Scott acted to quell the disturbance, imposing martial law on September 16. Putting teeth behind his words, he ordered his artillery to fire on houses from which gunfire came. Working with the *ayuntamiento* (city council), Scott brought an uneasy peace to the occupied capital.

Santa Anna had more than 9,000 troops still under his command as he prepared to abandon his nation's capital to Scott. He exited the city from the north and marched east to Puebla, where the small garrison left by Scott was under siege. The strategy was sound: sever Scott's link to the coast and prevent supplies and reinforcements from reaching him. Isolated in central Mexico, Scott's army would be reduced by natural attrition and vulnerable to popular uprisings. A threat in his rear might force Scott to withdraw from Mexico City. Even if it did not produce that result, a victory at Puebla would at least put Mexico in a better position to negotiate a favorable peace or perhaps even somehow turn the war in its favor.

Trouble for the garrison at Puebla had begun shortly after Scott's departure for the capital. Mexican patriots exhorted their fellow residents to action. Isolated American soldiers became targets. The agitation became bolder, with pamphlets appearing that encouraged resistance to the occupation. Some of the city's clergy provided leadership to the movement, often exhorting their compatriots to revolt. General Joaquín Rea, who commanded several thousand regular and irregular troops in the area, began to pressure the stranded garrison. Rea's men seized the quartermaster's mule herd and several bakeries supplying bread to the Americans. A series of coordinated attacks on the garrison's strongholds began on September 13. Although the garrison held on, the Americans faced constant small-arms firing over the next few weeks and were unable to leave their fortified positions.

Santa Anna arrived at Puebla on September 22 and assumed command of the siege. Fighting increased but the garrison held out, despite being overwhelmingly outnumbered by the combined armies of Santa Anna and Rea. Once again the Americans' artillery gave them the advantage. Commanding the city from its northern heights, the American gunners were able to see troops massing in the plazas and parks below and thereby break them up before they could begin to attack. The siege extended into October, and the continual warfare associated with this type of operation took a toll on the garrison. With no help from the outside, the garrison commander organized several companies of invalids from among the more than 2,000 hospital patients left by Scott and sent them to reinforce the front lines. A demand to surrender was refused. One Pennsylvanian recorded, "If Gen. Lane don't soon arrive to our relief, God only knows what will become of us, for we have resolved never to surrender, and the Mexicans have threatened that if we don't soon surrender they make this a second *Alamo*."[20] The implication of the threat was clear to the Americans, who understood the outcome if they did not hold out until help arrived.

Help was on the way for the embattled Puebla garrison. General Joseph Lane had left Vera Cruz on September 19 with reinforcements and supplies for Scott. He learned of the siege when he reached Plan del Rio. He attached other units from the vicinity of Perote to his column as he marched west over the National Road. One company that joined him was commanded by the former Texas Ranger Samuel H. Walker, serving as a captain in the U.S. Mounted Rifles. News reached Lane that Santa Anna had left Rea in charge of the siege and was leading his troops east to intercept the relief column before it reached Puebla. Lane decided to act first and, on October 9, placed his train under a strong guard and advanced on the village of Huamantla, where Santa Anna was reportedly massing his troops. Walker and his company led the way, outpacing Lane's infantry. Reaching the village ahead of the main column, Walker drove the Mexicans out. Quickly reorganizing, the Mexicans counterattacked and almost recaptured the village, killing Walker in the process. The death of the legendary officer enraged Lane's troops, who heard the sad news when they reached Huamantla. Mexican resistance was quickly overcome and the village sacked in retaliation. The destruction made an impression on Lieutenant A. P. Hill, future Confederate general, who later recalled, "Twas then I saw and felt how perfectly unmanageable volunteers were and how much damage they did."[21] Santa Anna, with his army in disarray, retreated to the countryside. Leaving Huamantla, Lane's column resumed its march, reaching Puebla on October 12 and ending the siege. The garrison had held on but at a cost of ninety-four killed, wounded, and missing.[22]

Scott's capture of Mexico City and Lane's relief of the besieged garrison at Puebla marked the end of the major operations of the war. Fighting continued but on a smaller scale, involving fewer combatants on both sides. Life for the Americans in Mexico settled down to the dull routine typically experienced by soldiers occupying a conquered country. Life for Mexicans settled down to that experienced by a people living under the watchful gaze of an occupying army. While life went on for both sides, the war entered a new phase in which the struggle was conducted by politicians and diplomats instead of generals and soldiers.

NOTES

1. James Longstreet, *From Manassas to Appomattox: Memoirs of the Civil War in America* (1896; Millwood, NY: Kraus Reprint, 1981), 20.
2. George Gordon Meade, *The Life and Letters of George Gordon Meade, Major-General United States Army* (New York: Charles Scribner's Sons, 1913), 1:80.

3. John Y. Simon, ed., *The Papers of Ulysses S. Grant, 1837–1861* (Carbondale: Southern Illinois University Press, 1967), 1:85.

4. Longstreet, *From Manassas to Appomattox*, 28.

5. John H. Schroeder, *Mr. Polk's War: American Opposition and Dissent, 1846–1848* (Madison: University of Wisconsin Press, 1973), 10–11.

6. [By an American Officer], *The National Songster* (New York: Cornish, Lamport, and Co., ca. 1848), 47–48.

7. Ibid., 83.

8. Ibid., 20–21.

9. William Elsey Connelley, *Doniphan's Expedition and the Conquest of New Mexico and California* (1848; Topeka: published by the author, 1907), 230.

10. Ibid., 232–233.

11. Rhoda van Bibber Tanner Doubleday, ed., *Journals of the Late Brevet Major Philip Norbourne Barbour and His Wife, Martha Isabella Hopkins Barbour* (New York: G. P. Putnam's Sons, 1936), 105–106.

12. Ibid., 107.

13. Manuel Balbotin, "The Siege of Monterrey," *Journal of the Military Service Institution of the United States* (1887), 325–354.

14. James Henry Carleton, *The Battle of Buena Vista, With the Operations of the "Army of Occupation" for One Month* (New York: Harper and Brothers, 1848), 36–37.

15. Manuel Balbotin, "The Battle of Angostura (Buena Vista)," *United State Cavalry Journal* (1894), 153–154.

16. William H. Richardson, "William H. Richardson's Journal of Doniphan's Expedition: Article Three," *Missouri Historical Review* (July 1928), 527.

17. Allan Peskin, ed., *Volunteers: The Mexican War Journals of Private Richard Coulter and Sergeant Thomas Barclay, Company E, Second Pennsylvania Infantry* (Kent, OH: Kent State University Press, 1991), 113.

18. Ibid.

19. Ibid.

20. J. Jacob Oswandel, *Notes of the Mexican War, 1846–47–48* (Philadelphia: n.p., 1885), 336.

21. James I. Robertson Jr., *General A. P. Hill: The Story of a Confederate Warrior* (New York: Random House, 1987), 15–17.

22. Long overshadowed by Scott's capture of Mexico City, the Siege of Puebla often is overlooked in histories of the war. For a study of the siege, see Richard Bruce Winders, "Puebla's Forgotten Heroes," *Military History of the West* (spring 1994), 1–23.

CHAPTER FIVE

ACT THREE
Conquering a Peace

Like all the guilty, *ad interim* President, Pena y Pena,
suffered from his conscience. Fearing what I might say
if he failed to issue me a passport, he granted me one.
He also gave me safe conduct from the invaders with
whom he was in league. Pena y Pena, who signed his
name to the *Treaty of Guadalupe Hidalgo,* will be forever
infamous in the memoirs of those Mexican patriots of
our times.
—Antonio López de Santa Anna
The Eagle (1888)

THE WAR WITH Mexico gave the United States the opportunity to fulfill its dream of Manifest Destiny. The desire for Texas had been a driving force throughout the 1830s and 1840s, but the annexation of Texas had finally been achieved. Was the time not right to acquire even more territory from Mexico while U.S. troops occupied her? Early in the war, talk began to be heard of making Mexico pay for the war by ceding her northern states.

Polk's strategy of sending armies as far as New Mexico and California reflected his expanded war aims. No longer would a clear title to Texas bounded by the Rio Grande on the south be sufficient. The problem he faced was that even though his generals had been victorious on all fronts, Mexico stubbornly refused to bring the war to a peaceful settlement. Although Mexico was rapidly overrun by enemy troops, powerful political elements still rejected the notion of surrender, knowing that it would be an admission that Texas—and perhaps much more—was lost. For this reason Mexican leaders continued to rebuild their shattered armies after each new defeat. But with their nation's capital occupied, the time had come to face the reality that Scott's victory had forced home.

Polk had been prepared to embrace a diplomatic settlement even as his armies marched across Mexico. What he, his advisers, and many of their countrymen could not understand was why the Mexicans were so obstinate. To his dismay, Taylor, Kearny, Frémont, and Stockton had dared to dabble in diplomatic endeavors on their own, granting armistices and making treaties without Polk's knowledge or consent. The entire outcome of the postwar settlement could be jeopardized by such independent maneuverings. For this reason, Polk sent an agent to Mexico to accompany Scott on his march to Mexico City. With his own man in place, Polk assumed that the war could be ended whenever the opportunity presented itself and on his terms.

The person selected for the task was Nicholas Trist, chief clerk of the State Department. His position, which sounds rather unimpressive, was the equivalent of a modern assistant secretary of state, making him second only to Secretary of State James Buchanan in the department's hierarchy. A career diplomat who spoke Spanish and had served for a time in Cuba, Trist had been a protégé of Thomas Jefferson. Highly cultured and intelligent, he seemed ideal for the post that was handed him on April 15, 1847.

Trist encountered unexpected resistance on his arrival at Vera Cruz in May 1847. Winfield Scott, the military commander in the theater, resented the diplomat's presence in Mexico, believing that as commander of the army he should be consulted on all matters involving the ultimate outcome of the war. Premature peace overtures might jeopardize the army's success. He further believed that Polk had sent Trist to Mexico to deny him the opportunity to handle the peace negotiations himself, something he felt perfectly qualified to do, having helped quell trouble with South Carolina during the Nullification Crisis in 1832 and again along the United States–Canada border during the Patriot disturbances of the late 1830s and early 1840s. Both Scott and Trist were haughty and arrogant in their initial dealings with one another, and both resolved to ignore the other. Each proceeded to carry out his respective mission without the other's aid. The impasse was broken when Scott sent a jar of marmalade to Trist, who had become ill. Won over by the simple gesture, Trist responded with an effusive note of thanks. The two men reconciled their differences and built a cordial relationship that lasted while they were together in Mexico, each becoming an ardent supporter of the other.

Trist received word through British diplomats in Mexico City in late June 1847 that Santa Anna might be receptive to peace under certain conditions. First, Scott's army must advance no further than Puebla. Second, a sum of money—possibly as high as a million dollars—would be needed to convince Mexican officials to accept peace. Although Scott and Trist agreed to the second stipulation, the negotiations broke down and Scott resumed his march on Mexico City.

The next chance for negotiation came on the heels of Scott's successes at Contreras and Churubusco on August 20, 1847. With U.S. troops poised to enter Mexico City, Scott and Santa Anna agreed to an armistice that went into effect on August 24, intended to give the Mexican government time to consider the new developments. Negotiations opened on August 27 when Trist met with José Ramón Pacheco, Mexico's foreign minister, and each presented his nation's proposed terms for peace. Trist relayed his administration's demand for the Rio Grande as the southern boundary of Texas and the cession of New Mexico and California as war indemnities. Pacheco offered to recognize the Nueces River as Texas's boundary but stated that giving up additional territory was out of the question.

More talks were conducted on September 1, 1847, once each side had had time to review and discuss the initial proposals. Trist, straying from the instructions given to him by Polk and Buchanan, offered to accept the Nueces as Texas's southern boundary if Mexico would cede Alta California and New Mexico. For its part, the United States would pay Mexico $30 million for the new territory it would receive. Pacheco replied with a counteroffer on September 5, stating that Mexico would cede northern California but not New Mexico. Violations of the armistice by the Mexican Army and the residents of Mexico City combined with the hard line taken by Pacheco prompted Scott to resume hostilities once the two-week truce ended.

Scott's occupation of the Mexican capital on September 14, 1847, greatly weakened the Mexican government's bargaining position. Although such radicals as Gómez Farías argued for continued resistance, moderates concluded that their nation's best interest would be served by ending the war. Manuel de la Peña y Peña, the presiding justice of the Supreme Court, headed an interim government. Convening at the town of Querétaro north of Mexico City, the Mexican Congress elected Pedro María Anaya president. President Anaya appointed Peña y Peña minister of foreign relations and Luis G. Cuevas, Bernardo Couto, and Miguel Atristain commissioners with authority to treat with Trist. Mexico finally was ready to sue for peace.

Ironically, the peace process now faced an obstacle from an unexpected quarter. On October 5, 1847, Polk, who was dissatisfied with the lack of diplomatic progress and uneasy over the cooperation between Scott and Trist, ordered Buchanan to instruct the chief clerk to break off any ongoing negotiations and immediately return to the United States. Trist received his new instructions in November 1847, just when it appeared that Mexico was ready to consent to Polk's demands. Seeking advice from his peers in Mexico City, Trist was encouraged by personal friends, foreign diplomats, Mexican officials, and even Scott to ignore his latest instructions, remain in Mexico, and continue negotiations. Trist explained his reason for disobeying his superiors, writing that officials in Washington did not know the true situations in Mexico and that negotiations, while possible now, would be unlikely if the radical element gained control of the Querétaro government. Polk was infuriated by what he considered Trist's insolence and treachery. The nature of nineteenth-century communications, however, provided his rogue diplomat with the time needed to complete negotiations with his Mexican counterparts and ultimately to secure a peace treaty.

Negotiations were conducted at the village of Guadalupe Hidalgo. The unusual situation convinced the Mexican commissioners to accept Polk's demand of establishing Texas's border at the Rio Grande as well as ceding both Alta California and New Mexico to the United States. For their part, the Mexican commissioners asked for the removal of all U.S. military and naval forces from its remaining territory as well as fair treatment of Mexican citizens within the territory ceded to the United States. These people would be allowed to choose whether to remain and become U.S. citizens or to move with their property to Mexico. The commissioners wanted guarantees that the people affected by the treaty would not suffer any financial loss or diminished legal standing and that their civil rights would be protected in the years to come. The treaty also made the United States responsible for controlling nomadic raiders such as the Comanche, who had warred against both Texas and Mexico. On his government's behalf, Trist offered to pay Mexico $15 million to indemnify the country for its ceded territory and to assume $3,250,000 in U.S. claims against Mexico. On February 2, 1848, representatives from both sides signed the agreement known as the Treaty of Guadalupe Hidalgo.

The document reached Washington in record time. Trist asked James L. Freaner, a correspondent for the *New Orleans Delta* who had become a close confidant, to deliver the treaty personally to Secretary of State Buchanan. Freaner left the Mexican capital on February 3, just one day after the treaty had been signed. He pushed on to Vera Cruz, sometimes riding alone through stretches still controlled by guerrillas and bandits, making the trip in just three days. Officials at the port, whom Freaner told of his mission, ordered the U.S. steamer *Iris* to carry the courier to Mobile, Alabama. Back on U.S. soil, Freaner traveled by rail to Washington, DC, arriving on the night of February 19, 1848. He had made the 2,000-mile journey in just over two weeks.

Polk faced a difficult choice. The treaty clearly had been concluded by an official whose authority to represent the United States had been revoked. He had every right as president to reject the treaty outright. Polk's dilemma was that Trist had achieved almost everything originally sought from Mexico. Recommending the illegitimate treaty to the Senate would bring the war to a successful conclusion; rejecting the treaty would mean a costly and prolonged occupation of Mexico and continued discord in the U.S. Congress. After meeting with his cabinet for two days (February 20 and 21) to discuss the matter, Polk sent the treaty on to the Senate on February 23 with his recommendation for its passage.

The debate in the Senate reflected divisions within the U.S. Congress and the nation. Opponents of slavery opposed any territorial acquisition, especially without a ban on the institution in land ceded by Mexico. Some proslavery senators tried to block the treaty because they believed that the United States was entitled to even more land than Trist had obtained. The death of the venerated John Q. Adams at the height of the debate interrupted the wrangling. Urged by Polk to accept the treaty, the Senate ratified it with his requested revisions on March 10, 1848, in a vote of thirty-eight to fourteen.

Returned to Mexico, the treaty came before the Mexican Congress. Radicals opposed the treaty on the grounds that continued resistance eventually would result in a treaty more favorable to

Mexico. Moderates argued that Mexico had suffered enough and that peace was needed before the country could again experience prosperity. The radicals viewed Mexico's loss of New Mexico and California as a disaster, explaining that the rich territory was critical to their nation's future. Moderates countered by emphasizing the great distance between the capital and these borderlands as well as their sparse populations: Divesting itself of this empty space would allow the nation to expend its resources on more populous and productive regions. Moreover, pointing to the expansionist mood of the United States, the moderates contended that the United States would demand even more territory if forced to reopen negotiations. The treaty passed both houses of the Mexican Congress and was signed into law on May 25, 1848. Five days later, newspaper headlines in Mexico City announced that the war between the United States and Mexico was officially over.

One occupation newspaper, the *American Star,* offered its readers the following words in its final issue:

> FAREWELL TO MEXICO. The great mission for which the American Army entered the capital has been accomplished. Peace is proclaimed—the war is at an end. General Scott's idea of "conquering a peace," has at length been realized, and we are all on the march for the coast. Many of the troops will return to their homes, and talk over with families and friends, the perils of the camp. Others will repair to the delightful shores of Yucatan, to give a helping hand to the white inhabitants of that Peninsula, in their desperate struggle with the Indians.[1]

Thus, even as one conflict came to a close the editors hinted that others were on the horizon.

American troops soon began marching toward their respective points of embarkation: Point Isabel for northern Mexico and Vera Cruz for central Mexico. The men of the artillery battalions who had served as infantry returned to their permanent garrisons in the forts along the Atlantic and Gulf Coasts. The rest of the regular troops prepared to move to their new posts in Texas, Oregon, New Mexico, and California. The army of volunteers returned to their various states where they were mustered out of federal service. One regiment of New York Volunteers, however, had been raised for the express purpose of settling California and therefore were disbanded in their new home. Also mustered out in California were two battalions of Mormon Volunteers, who had agreed to help occupy the region as part of their terms of enlistment. By October 1848 the nation had demobilized and was making the effort to return to life as it had been before the war.

Mexico's defeated leader, Santa Anna, prepared to enter exile once more. An escort of U.S. troops were provided to see that he had safe passage out of the country, unmolested by Americans or Mexicans who may have held a grudge against him. Near Jalapa, the party had an unexpected encounter with men who had reason to seek revenge on the defeated man. The coach had stopped so the travelers could rest and eat, when the escort's commander learned that a battalion of Texas Volunteers—Jack Hays's men—were nearby. The famous Texan entered the house where Santa Anna was taking refreshments. Wrote Major John R. Kenly of what followed:

> I noticed Colonel Hays. I rose from the table, and approaching the colonel, who was dressed as usual, with a round jacket, Mexican hat, and no badge of rank other than a silk sash tied around his waist after the fashion of the Mexicans, said to him, "Suppose you let me present you to General Santa Anna"; he said, "Well," and we walked toward the head table. As we approached him there was general suspension of conversation, a movement of alarm was perceived among the Mexican officers of the escort, and a silence very painful to me pervaded the hall. Santa Anna was eating fruit. I said, "General, permit me to present to you"—when I had got thus far, he turned his face toward us and was in the act of rising— "Colonel Jack Hays." When I pronounced this name, his whole appearance and demeanor changed, and if a loaded bombshell, with fuse burning and sputtering, had fallen on that dinner table, a greater sensation would not have been caused.[2]

With the Mexican officers and Mrs. Santa Anna watching to see what would happen, Santa Anna sat back down and resumed eating fruit without looking up. Hays quietly withdrew from the room, and soon afterward Santa Anna and his party announced that they were ready to go, a decision based on the knowledge that there were Texans nearby. When the coach passed by the encampment of Hays's men, they found that the Texans silently lined the road but made no attempt to harm the party. "The Texans had behaved with great propriety, the well-disposed among them checking even an utterance of what might have been deemed disrespectful, to one under the safeguard and honor of our flag."[3]

As unlikely as it seemed at the time, Santa Anna would serve as Mexico's leader once again. In 1853 he returned from exile in the Caribbean and was granted dictatorial power with which to restore order to a war-torn nation. The need for money to ensure the army's loyalty caused Santa Anna to approve the sale of the Mesilla Valley, an act known in the United States as the Gadsden Purchase. Outrage over the loss of yet more Mexican territory cost Santa Anna support from many quarters and ultimately led to his final ouster in 1855. He spent the next twenty years in exile, only returning to Mexico in 1874. He died two years later, remembered in the United States as the general who captured the Alamo and in his country as the man who lost Texas.

Mexico continued on without Santa Anna. In the 1850s, war erupted between liberals and conservatives in a conflict called the War of the Reform. Many of Mexico's old leaders had passed from the political scene. One of the new leaders who rose to power was Benito Juárez, a liberal from Oaxaca. In 1862, Juárez led resistance to a revival of the old plan voiced in the 1821 Plan de Igula that would impose a monarchy on the nation. Mexican monarchists, backed by the French, placed Austrian nobleman Maximilian on the throne once occupied by Agustín de Iturbide. Mexico's second empire, however, fared no better than its first. With the loss of French support, the monarchists could not sustain Maximilian, who was captured and executed on June 19, 1867. With external threats finally ended, Mexico under Juárez began to experience the first true peace it had known since independence.

The Mexican War left an indelible mark on both Mexico and the United States. Mexican leaders used the experience to forge a sense of unity that enabled them to begin the process of nation building. The conflict had the opposite effect on the United States as it began a rapid descent into civil war. Ironically, war with its old colonial rival, Spain, in 1898 helped to bind wounds suffered in the War Between the States.

Ample evidence indicates that the United States war with Mexico made a lasting impression on those Americans who participated in this pivotal event. Addressing a group of Indiana veterans in 1876 author Lew Wallace, who had served in Mexico as a young lieutenant before rising to the rank of general in the Union Army, told the gathering of aging men: "I venture to assert that there is not one of us to whom the service in Mexico is not a recollection surpassing in interest the most brilliant operation of the Rebellion." He explained his position, saying "Mexico was a strange land to us and full of novelties."[4] As compared to America's national tragedy that followed in the Mexican War's wake, the camps and battlefields of Mexico appeared to many Americans such as Wallace as bittersweet memories of an innocent age long lost.

NOTES

1. *The American Star* (Mexico City), May 30, 1848. For a study of the uprising in the Yucatán mentioned in the editorial, see Nelson Reed, *The Caste War of Yucatán* (n.p., 1964).

2. John R. Kenly, *Memoirs of a Maryland Volunteer* (Philadelphia: n.p., 1873), 394–397.

3. Ibid.

4. Lew Wallace, *Lew Wallace: An Autobiography*, 2 vols. (New York: Harper and Brothers Publishers, 1904), 2:895–896.

CHAPTER SIX

ENCORE
Setting the Stage for Crisis

As Pandora raised the lid, the cottage grew very dark
and dismal; for the black cloud had now swept quite
over the sun, and seemed to have buried it alive. There
had, for a little while past, been a low growling and
muttering, which all at once broke into a heavy peal of
thunder. But Pandora, heeding nothing of all this, lifted
the lid nearly upright, and looked inside. It seemed as
if a sudden swarm of winged creatures brushed past
her, taking flight out of the box, while, at the same
instant, she heard the voice of Epimetheus, with a
lamentable tone, as if he were in pain.

"Oh, I am stung!" cried he, "I am stung! Naughty
Pandora! Why have you opened this wicked box?"
—Nathaniel Hawthorne
A Wonder Book (1851)

ONE CRISIS WAS solved—or was it? The struggle for Texas, even
though ultimately successful, proved so contentious as to bring
about the dissolution of the Union that Americans had fought so
doggedly to create with Texas. By 1861, Texas had joined other
Southern states that were asserting their right to leave the federal
union. It is not too presumptuous to contend that the Civil War—
truly a war between the states—began with the ratification of the
Treaty of Guadalupe Hidalgo.

Slavery had become inexorably linked to the war with Mexico.
The connection was its extension into new territory gained from the
conflict. The Missouri Compromise had supposedly settled the slavery issue in 1820 by limiting its spread to U.S. territory south of the
line of latitude 30 degrees 36 minutes. Above the line, slavery would
be permitted only in Missouri. The law had also established the

WYOMING

**TEXAS TERRITORY
CEDED IN THE
COMPROMISE OF 1850**

COLORADO

KANSAS

NEW
MEXICO

OKLAHOMA

TEXAS

Map created for the Alamo
by Donald S. Frazier, Ph.D.

principle of preserving a balance of power between the free states and the slave states. The admission of Texas into the Union upset that balance. Moreover, the cession by Mexico of New Mexico, California, and other territory made the extension of slavery into newly acquired lands located south of the Missouri Compromise line a real possibility, rekindling the smoldering debate.

The question of slavery was dramatically injected into the debate over the war by Representative David Wilmot, a Democrat from Pennsylvania. On August 8, 1846, the House began discussing Polk's request for $2 million to be used to fund peace negotiations with Mexico. The money was to be offered in exchange for a favorable boundary settlement that included recognition of the Rio Grande as Texas's border and, if possible, the acquisition of California as well. Wilmot began by saying that unlike some in the House, he believed the current war was "necessary and proper."[1] He then voiced his reservation over acceding to the president's wishes: "We claim the Rio Grande as our boundary—that was the main cause of the war. Are we now to purchase what we claim as a matter of right?" He further contended that he was not opposed to extending U. S. boundaries to the Pacific Ocean, "provide it were done on proper conditions." Any new territory gained from Mexico, however, must be free of the South's "peculiar institution." He defended his vote in favor of Texas's annexation, making the distinction that slavery had already existed there. Toward the end of the debate, Wilmot moved that the following amendment be added to the appropriation bill:

> *Provided,* That, as an express and fundamental condition to the acquisition of any territory from the Republic of Mexico by the Unites States, by virtue of any treaty which may be negotiated between them, and to the use of the Executive of the money herein appropriated, neither slavery nor involuntary servitude shall ever exist in any part of said territory, except for crime, whereof the party shall first be duly convicted.[2]

The amendment passed but not without stiff opposition.

The Wilmot Proviso was eventually stricken from the bill, but proponents repeatedly attached it to subsequent war appropriations. Though doomed to fail each time it came up, the amendment provided a handy tool by which the antislavery faction in the House could express its view, sometimes in a most dramatic way. During the original debate on the amendment, John Quincy Adams—elder statesman of the Whig Party and staunch opponent of slavery—compared Mexico to a slave that had been punished by his master: "Sir, we have whipped her more already than the most cruel task-master ever whipped a slave, without cause and without necessity. I see no reason for whipping Mexico more than we have done."[3]

The Whigs used debate on wartime legislation to attack Polk and the Democrats at every opportunity. In one of the more memorable opposition speeches of the war, Ohio's Senator Thomas Corwin challenged the accuracy of Polk's claim that "American blood had been shed on the American soil," contending that Mexico was the aggrieved party in the current conflict. He proclaimed, "If I were a Mexican I would tell you, 'Have you not room in your own country to bury your dead men? If you come into mine, we will greet you with bloody hands, and welcome you to hospitable graves.'"[4] Illinois Whig Abraham Lincoln brought the issue of Polk's claim to the House of Representatives, introducing the "spot resolution," which challenged the president to prove that the war had commenced on American soil and not in Mexico.[5] Although the heated rhetoric failed to stop the U.S. Congress from funding the war, remarks such as these kept the parties locked in verbal combat.

Even though some in the U.S. Congress complained that the United States was imposing too high a price for peace in Mexico, others countered that the nation was due even more land than that sought by Polk. By late 1847 a call was heard for the United States to claim the entire country of Mexico as punishment for the trouble that nation had caused and as an indemnity for the cost of engaging the United States in war. The All-of-Mexico Movement, as the plan was called, was as strongly opposed as it was supported. Opponents pointed to the dubious contention that Mexico lay at fault for the war as well as to the severity of the claim. The slavery issue also entered into the debate, with both abolitionists and some of the institution's strongest supporters actually joining together to argue against annexing all of Mexico to the Union. Abolitionist forces based their opposition on the desire to curtail the extension of slavery. The proslavery faction, headed by South Carolinian John C. Calhoun, opposed the plan not only because it believed that slavery was unsuited for parts of Mexico but also because it feared the effect that bringing in a large population so different in culture, ethnicity, and religion would have on the United States republican institutions. The signing of the Treaty of Guadalupe Hidalgo ended the debate, at least for the moment; the desire for more territory would resurface in the guise of filibustering expeditions around the Caribbean in the 1850s.

The strain caused by the war proved too much for the Jacksonian party system, which started to break apart even with peace finally in sight. During such trying times as the annexation debate the Democrats and Whigs were able to cross sectional lines and maintain national constituencies. Representatives and senators alike, with very few exceptions, voted along straight party lines on the joint resolution admitting Texas to the Union. But the question of whether to allow slavery to spread to new territories shattered old alliances. Voting on the Wilmot Proviso fell along sectional lines each time it came before the House or Senate. U.S. congressmen began to form regional alliances. The Whig Party, for example, developed distinct sectional factions. Northern Whigs became known as Conscience Whigs because of their opposition to slavery, whereas Southern Whigs became known as Cotton Whigs because of their defense of the institution. Although nominally from the same party, the Northern and Southern Whigs increasingly found themselves on opposite sides of national issues. The Democrats also divided along sectional lines, although their disintegration as a national party took longer to complete.

Polk and his administration found themselves at war with not just Mexico but with Northern Whigs and Democrats. In political battles, patronage often proves to be the ultimate weapon. Secretary of War William L. Marcy, who coined the political adage "to the victor go the spoils," assisted Polk in using military commissions and assignments as a way to reward supporters and punish enemies. When Polk assumed office, many of the army's top staff officers were Whigs. Once the war began, Polk believed that he could not rely on the old establishment to fulfill his objectives. The creation of new regular regiments and the raising of state volunteers enabled him to appoint loyal Democrats to the army's higher echelon. The mobilization created positions for thirteen generals to command the volunteers: Polk filled each of these vacancies with a Democratic politician, even offering a general's star to Senator Samuel Houston of Texas and Senator Jefferson Davis of Mississippi (fresh from the battlefield of Buena Vista), both of whom declined. Polk also granted commissions to loyal Democrats, trusted men who would officer the newly raised regular regiments at every level. Thus, the military took on a decidedly Democratic complexion owing to Polk's actions.

The president also warred with his top commanders, Zachary Taylor and Winfield Scott. Both Old Rough and Ready and Old Fuss and Feathers, as the two generals were respectively called by their men and the American public, were Whigs. Their victories on the battlefield enhanced their popularity and made them attractive candidates for the White House in the approaching 1848 presidential election. Polk had believed that he could secure Taylor's loyalty by rewarding his successes at Palo Alto and Resaca de La Palma with a promotion to major general. Shortly thereafter, though, Taylor's name began to appear in the nation's press as a likely presidential candidate, and the general did little to dispel the notion. His armistice with Ampudia at Monterrey gave Polk the justification he needed to divert attention from Taylor by shifting the theater of operations to another region, thereby hopefully depriving the general of the limelight. Taylor complained that Polk had set him up for defeat in order to lessen his chances of becoming president. However, his underdog victory at Buena Vista made Taylor an even bigger hero than before.

Polk never held any notions that he could make an ally of Scott. Possessing the vanity that comes with uncommon achievement, Scott had held the rank of general for most of his adult life. The president and Scott clashed soon after hostilities commenced. Scott, commanding general of the army, expected to be called on to provide the guiding hand in his nation's war against Mexico, but Polk did not want Scott's help. When the general inadvertently insulted the president and the secretary of war by telling Marcy, "I do not desire to place myself in the most perilous of all positions;—*a fire upon my rear, from Washington, and the fire in front, from the Mexicans*," Polk reprimanded Scott and made it clear that there was no place in the war for him.[6]

The lack of progress in northern Mexico changed the situation. Before being set aside by the administration, Scott had been working on a plan to bring Mexico to the peace table by landing an army at Vera Cruz, marching inland, and seizing Mexico City. Even Scott's detractors had to admit that the general was undoubtedly the nation's leading expert on military matters and that there was indeed a role for him in the current conflict. Polk grudgingly asked Scott to put the Vera Cruz plan into effect, placing the general in charge of the campaign.

The relationship between the president and his top general quickly soured. Polk voiced his distrust of Scott even before the expedition got under way. The arrival of Nicholas P. Trist in Mexico, vested with the authority to broker a peace treaty, convinced Scott that Polk intended to undermine his chances for personal advancement that might result from any success he might achieve. Even Scott's spectacular capture of Mexico City did not shield him from the president's invective order recalling him from Mexico to answer charges levied against him by one of Polk's Democratic generals, Gideon J. Pillow. Thus, in late February 1848 the nation's most successful commander since George Washington sailed home under a dark cloud to face a court of inquiry orchestrated by his political enemies. Scott's successor was Major General William O. Butler, another of Polk's Democratic appointees.

The presidential election of 1848 revealed the shifting tides in national politics created by the war. The Whigs turned to Zachary Taylor, the Hero of Buena Vista, to win the White House for them. Polk, who had campaigned on the pledge to serve only one term if elected, could not be enticed to abandon his promise. Denied the power of an incumbent president, mainstream Democrats selected War of 1812 veteran and former Secretary of War Lewis Cass to carry their banner. These candidates' respective running mates were Millard Fillmore and William O. Butler. A third party, the Free Soil Party, composed of disaffected Northern Whigs and Democrats, entered the race during this campaign. Martin Van Buren, who resented being denied the Democratic nomination four years earlier, received the new party's nomination. Taylor's popularity won the day as the Whigs capitalized on what had essentially been a war brought on and conducted by the Democrats. A deciding factor in Taylor's win had been the defection of northern Democrats to Van Buren, votes that otherwise would have gone to Cass.

Whig presidents seemed to be cursed, as both William Henry Harrison and Zachary Taylor were destined to die in office. Death came to Old Rough and Ready in July 1850 at the height of debate over the extension of slavery into the newly acquired western lands.

Taylor's successor was Vice President Millard Fillmore, who, like John Tyler before him, also failed to receive his party's support, which would have allowed him to run for his own term. The presidential contest of 1852 pitted two military chieftains against one another for the nation's top office. The Whigs finally turned to Winfield Scott. Polk's fear had been realized, although he did not live to see the outcome. The Democrats nominated Franklin Pierce, yet another of Polk's volunteer generals. The Free Soilers again entered the fray but stood no real chance of winning, although they continued to serve as a reminder of the fracturing of old alliances. Scott's pomposity overshadowed his positive attributes, and Pierce won the 1852 race.

The war's shadow still hung over the presidential election of 1856. James Buchanan, Polk's secretary of war, received the Democratic nomination. The Whig Party had finally succumbed to the internal and external strife that had been pulling it apart and, for the first time since 1840, failed to field a presidential candidate. The Free Soil Party also fielded no candidate, but two new parties appeared on the political scene to take their places. One, called the American Native Party or the Know Nothings, courted Sam Houston but backed former Vice President Millard Fillmore. The Know Nothings reflected the growing nativist sentiment. The other new party, called the Republicans, picked John C. Frémont of California fame as their candidate. The Republican Party was the new home of Free Soilers, Conscience Whigs, and antislavery Democrats and, as such, clearly represented the abolitionist bloc within the nation. Although the Democrats triumphed in the election, it proved to be the last victory of the party founded by Jackson.

Interestingly, Mexico's defeat brought Texas into potential conflict with the United States ten years before the coming of the Civil War. The point of contention was once again Texas's boundary. The United States and Texas had clashed before over the boundary in 1843 when the republic's president, Sam Houston, sanctioned raids along the Santa Fe Trail designed to interfere with Mexican commerce. U.S. troops, who encountered a band of Texans under the command of Jacob Snively operating along the Arkansas River, disarmed the raiders and sent them back to Texas. After the signing of the Treaty of Guadalupe Hidalgo, Texas officials sought to uphold the republic's claim that their state actually extended westward to the Rio Grande. In 1848 the Texas legislature passed an act organizing New Mexico into Santa Fe County. New Mexicans, however, wanted to be allowed to form their own territory separate from Texas. President Zachary Taylor and his administration supported New Mexico's claim to self-rule. By 1850 it appeared that the issue might have to be resolved by a clash of arms as both Texas and the United States threatened to use force. The Texas border issue was defused by the group of acts known collectively as the Compromise of 1850. The state, faced with the financial debts left over from the republic, was convinced to cede its disputed western land to the United States in exchange for $10 million. The new northern and western boundaries, as set forth by the bill, left Texas with the political outline it retains today.

The decade of the 1850s provided no relief for the strife-torn nation. Proslavery and antislavery factions continued to battle in the U.S. Congress and the popular press. The battle of Kansas saw both parties resorting to the practices that had worked so well against Spain and Mexico, as each sent an army of filibusters to impose its ideology on the territory. Political parties continued to rip asunder, with the Democrats formally splitting along sectional lines in 1860, a divide that had actually formed several years earlier. With the election of the Republican candidate Abraham Lincoln, Texas once again viewed itself as about to fall under the heels of a tyrant.

After only nineteen years, delegates gathered in Austin to undo what had been so hard-won—annexation. The strain between sectional factions had become too great to be resolved by compromise any longer. Voting to secede from the Union, the delegates explained that the action was taken because the government of the United States had failed to make the Texas frontier safe from the Comanche, who had resumed their attacks on the Texans as new settlements moved westward. As important as was that factor, another actually proved more forceful. The assembly declared that the Northern states, through the federal government, were attempting to force their will on Southern states such as Texas. The delegates evidently were compelled to explain their action to the world and, like the Texas revolutionaries of 1835 who had fought against Mexico's centralist government, they issued their own Declaration of Causes. Annexation, which had been approved by a plebiscite, was repealed subsequently by the same device by a vote of 46,129 to 14,697. By passing the repeal measure, Texans endorsed Texas's Ordinance of Secession, which read in part:

> We, the People of the State of Texas, by delegates in Convention assembled, do declare and ordain, that the ordinance adopted by our convention of delegates, on the 4th day of July, A.D. 1845, and afterward ratified by us, under which the Republic of Texas was admitted into union with other States and became a party to the compact styled "The Constitution of the United States of America" be and is hereby repealed and annulled.[7]

Thus, the first State of Texas was no more.

Texans had finally accepted and embraced Mirabeau B. Lamar's vision of Texas by choosing to build an empire clear to the Pacific Ocean. Within months, an army of Texans had returned to New Mexico to reclaim this lost territory. The former Texas president, however, had already passed from the scene, dying at his home in Richmond, Texas, in 1859 at the age of sixty-seven.

For Sam Houston, the reversal was especially painful, as it fell to Old San Jacinto, then governor of Texas, to help lead his state out of the Union. He told friends that he declined an offer from Abraham Lincoln to send 70,000 troops to Texas to counter the secessionists because he believed the use of force would only speed the nation's rush to civil war. Once secession was accomplished, however, Houston refused to take an oath to the Confederacy, prompting the secessionist legislature to expel him from office. Justifying his stance, he told his fellow Texans:

> I have declared my determination to stand by Texas in whatever position she assumes. Her people have declared in favor of separation from the Union. I have followed her banners before, when in exile from the land of my fathers. I went back into the Union with the people of Texas. I go out from the Union with them; and though I see only gloom before me, I shall follow the "Lone Star" with the same devotion as of yore.[8]

So did thousands of other Texans, many the veterans of previous conflicts with Mexico.

NOTES

1. *Congressional Globe*, August 8, 1846, 1214, 1216, 1217.
2. Ibid.

3. Ibid.

4. "Speech of Mr. Corwin, of Ohio, on the Mexican War" (delivered in the Senate of the United States, February 11, 1847), 13.

5. John H. Schroeder, *Mr. Polk's War: American Opposition and Dissent, 1846–1848* (Madison: University of Wisconsin Press, 1973), 153.

6. Timothy D. Johnson, *Winfield Scott: The Quest for Military Glory* (Lawrence: University Press of Kansas, 1998), 154.

7. Ernest Wallace, David M. Vigness, and George B. Ward, eds., *Documents of Texas History*, 2d ed. (Austin: State House Press, 1994), 194.

8. Amelia Williams and Eugene C. Barker, eds., *The Writing of Sam Houston, 1813–1863* (Austin: University of Texas Press, 1938), 8:275.

BIBLIOGRAPHICAL ESSAY

A comprehensive reading list for this time period would itself fill a volume. Therefore, the following works are those that I have found particularly useful and will serve to acquaint the student or general reader with key authors who have made significant historiographical contributions to topics discussed in this study.

Understanding the ideology of American expansionism is key. Two older studies, Norman A. Graebner's *Empire on the Pacific: A Study in American Continental Expansion* (1955) and Frederick Merk's *Manifest Destiny and Mission in American History* (1963), serve as excellent introductions. Readers are encouraged also to see these other important works in this field: Reginald Horsman, *Race and Manifest Destiny* (1981); Thomas R. Hietala, *Manifest Design: Anxious Aggrandizement in Late Jacksonian America* (1985); and Anders Stephenson, *Manifest Destiny: American Expansion and the Empire of Right* (1995).

Several works deal specifically with the topic of American filibusters in Spanish Texas. The most recent is a broad examination of attempts by the United States to acquire the Spanish Gulf Coast. Frank Lawrence Owsley Jr. and Gene A. Smith offer evidence in *Filibusters and Expansionists: Jeffersonian Manifest Destiny, 1800–1821* (1997) that the American desire to possess North America began long before the term was coined by John L. O'Sullivan in 1845. Ted Schwarz and Robert H. Thonhoff chronicle the Gutiérrez-Magee Expedition of 1812–13 in their work *Forgotten Battlefield of the First Texas Revolution* (1985). Two older studies, Julia Kathryn Garrett's *Green Flag over Texas: A Story of the Last Years of Spain in Texas* (1939) and Harris Gaylord Warren's *The Sword Was Their Passport: A History of American Filibustering in the Mexican Revolution* (1943), are still valuable reading. For an insight into Spanish Texas prior to the filibustering campaigns, see Felix D. Almaráz Jr.'s *Tragic Cavalier: Governor Manuel Salcedo of Texas, 1808–1813* (1971).

The story of colonization is best told through biographical treatments of Stephen F. Austin. For many years, Eugene C. Barker's *Life of Stephen F. Austin* (1925) has been the standard work on Texas's most influential *empresario*. This early Texas historian produced an impressive number of articles dealing with Texas's colonization and revolt, many of which appeared in the *Southwestern Historical Quarterly* and its predecessor, *Quarterly of the Texas State Historical Association*. A serious challenge to Barker's study of Austin is a recent biography by Gregg Cantrell, *Stephen F. Austin: Empresario of Texas* (1999).

The Texas Revolution does not lack for historians. William C. Binkley's collection of essays, *The Texas Revolution* (1952), presents an excellent overview of the ideological issues behind the conflict. Seldom does such a thin volume as this contain such a broad explanation of an important historical event. The 1832 disturbances that prefaced the revolt are illuminated by Margaret Swett Henson in *Juan Davis Bradburn: A Reappraisal of the Mexican Commander of Anahuac* (1982). Alwyn Barr discusses the campaign to drive the Mexican Army out of Béxar in *Texans in Revolt: The Battle for San Antonio, 1835* (1990). Those interested in the military aspects of the revolution should see Stephen L. Hardin's *Texian Iliad: A Military History of the Texas Revolution 1835–1836* (1994). Readers interested in an intellectual history of the revolt are directed to Paul D. Lack, *The Texas Revolutionary Experience: A Political and Social History, 1835–1836* (1992).

As well-known as the Texas Revolution is, those conducting the revolt have largely gone unstudied. Part of this neglect can be attributed to the fascination with James Bowie, David Crockett, Sam Houston, and William B. Travis. Unfortunately, much of what has been written about these men and other Anglo participants is a mixture of fact and legend. It is hoped that William C. Davis's *Three Roads to the Alamo: The Lives and Fortunes of David Crockett, James Bowie, and William Barret Travis* (1998) will serve as a model to future scholars who want to study other less prominent participants. A useful study for understanding the world of Tejano participants is Andrés Tijerina's *Tejanos and Texas under the Mexican Flag, 1821–1836* (1994).

As in the case of colonization, the history of the Republic of Texas sometimes is told best through the lives of its leaders. Sam Houston, the republic's most noted citizen, has received more attention than his contemporaries. Two biographies have proven themselves classics: Marquis James, *The Raven: A Biography of Sam Hous-*

ton (1929), and Lierena B. Friend, *Sam Houston: The Great Designer* (1954). Both contain a decidedly pro-Houston interpretation of Texas history. Although more recent works have appeared, they have failed to replace either James or Friend. Mirabeau B. Lamar has also had his biographies, the most scholarly of which is Stanley Siegel's *The Poet President of Texas: The Life of Mirabeau B. Lamar* (1977). One of the most interesting books on a political figure from the Republic of Texas is Herbert Gambrell's *Anson Jones: The Last President of Texas* (1948). John H. Jenkins's biography *Edward Burleson: Texas Frontier Leader* (1990) explores the life of a figure whose importance often is overlooked. Some authors have concentrated on Texans other than presidents. Fayette Copeland examines the life of George W. Kendall in *Kendall of the Picayune, Being His Adventures in New Orleans, on the Texan Santa Fe Expedition, in the Mexican War, and in the Colonization of the Texas Frontier* (1943). Paul N. Spellman's *Forgotten Texas Leader: Hugh McLeod and the Texan Santa Fe Expedition* (1999) presents readers with a much-needed assessment of the commander of the Santa Fe Pioneers.

The 10-year-long conflict between Texas and Mexico, although it has not gone undocumented, has failed to be incorporated into mainstream Texas history. Two volumes by Joseph Milton Nance, *After San Jacinto: The Texas-Mexican Frontier, 1836–1841* (1963) and *Attack and Counterattack: The Texas-Mexican Frontier, 1842* (1964), are a wealth of information, but many readers find these massive works too daunting to tackle. Nance was unable to complete a volume on the Mier Expedition before his death; Archie P. McDonald edited Nance's unfinished manuscript and oversaw its publication as *Dare-Devils All: The Texan Mier Expedition, 1842–1844* (1998). Sam W. Haynes's *Soldiers of Misfortune: The Somervell and Mier Expeditions* (1990) provides a highly readable explanation of this episode and its consequences. Those interested in firsthand accounts are directed to George Wilkins Kendall, *Narrative of the Texan Santa Fé Expedition* (1844), and Thomas Jefferson Green, *Journal of the Texian Expedition against Mier* (1845). Although the experiences have been penned by other participants of the expeditions, Kendall and Green are the best known outside Texas history. One other work that is useful to students of Texas military history is Gerald S. Pierce's *Texas under Arms: The Camps, Posts, Forts, and Military Towns of the Republic of Texas, 1836–1846* (1969).

Various aspects of life in the Republic of Texas can be found in the following works: Donaly E. Brice's *The Great Comanche Raid: Boldest Indian Attack of the Texas Republic* (1987) discusses relations between Texans and the Comanche that culminated in the Battle of Plum Creek. Rena Maverick Green provides readers with a woman's point of view in the edited work, *Memoirs of Mary A. Maverick* (1921). Paul Mitchell Marks also explores Mary Maverick and her more famous husband in *Turn Your Eyes Toward Texas: Pioneers Sam and Mary Maverick* (1989). William Ransom Hogan's *The Texas Republic: A Social and Economic History* (1946) should be considered standard reading for any student of Texas history. Randolph B. Campbell's study, *An Empire for Slavery: The Peculiar Institution in Texas, 1821–1865* (1989), explores this important aspect of Texas history.

The story of Texas's annexation to the United States is woven throughout the biographies of those who participated in the event. David M. Pletcher's *The Diplomacy of Annexation: Texas, Oregon, and the Mexican War* (1973) continues to serve as the standard authority on the subject. *James K. Polk and the Expansionist Impulse* (1996) by Sam W. Haynes provides a brief but clear introduction to Polk and his role in expanding the United States boundaries.

The literature on the Mexican War is more voluminous than most readers imagine. One of my personal favorite general histories of the conflict is *The Story of the Mexican War* (1950) by Robert Selph Henry. Another excellent overview of the war is K. Jack Bauer's *The Mexican War, 1846–1848* (1974). Two works on the war that provide perspective on the American participants are James M. McCaffrey's *Army of Manifest Destiny: The American Soldier in the Mexican War, 1846–1848* (1992) and Richard B. Winders's *Mr. Polk's Army: The American Military Experience in the Mexican War* (1997). *To the Halls of the Montezumas: The Mexican War in the American Imagination* (1985) by Robert Johannsen explores how Americans of the period viewed the conflict and how it affected their world. An excellent collection of soldiers' accounts can be found in George Winston Smith and Charles Judah, eds., *Chronicles of the Gringos* (1968).

Studies of generals who led American forces to victory have been few. For many years Charles Winslow Elliott's *Winfield Scott: The Soldier and the Man* (1937) remained the classic work on Scott. Two new biographies have recently appeared: John S. D. Eisenhower's *Agent of Destiny: The Life and Times of General Winfield Scott* (1997) and Timothy D. Johnson's *Winfield Scott: The Quest for Military*

Glory (1998). Of the two, Johnson presents a fresher interpretation of Scott. The best biography on Taylor is K. Jack Bauer's *Zachary Taylor: Soldier, Planter, Statesman of the Old Southwest* (1985). Few biographers have taken as their subject the lieutenants of Scott and Taylor. Three notable exceptions are Edward S. Wallace's *General William Jenkins Worth: Monterey's Forgotten Hero* (1953), Robert E. May's *John A. Quitman: Old South Crusader* (1985), and Nathaniel Cheairs Hughes Jr. and Roy P. Stonesifer Jr.'s *The Life and Wars of Gideon J. Pillow* (1993). Two studies of other important officers include Joseph E. Chance's *Jefferson Davis's Mexican War Regiment* (1991) and Roger D. Launius's *Alexander William Doniphan: Portrait of a Missouri Moderate* (1997). Two works on important Texas military chieftains are James K. Greer's *Texas Ranger: Jack Hays in the Frontier Southwest* (1993) and Thomas W. Cutrer's *Ben McCulloch and the Frontier Military Tradition* (1993).

Several historians have chosen to study the Treaty of Guadalupe Hidalgo and Nicholas P. Trist. *The Treaty of Guadalupe Hidalgo: A Legacy of Conflict* (1990) by Richard Griswold del Castillo studies the document's origins, negotiations, adoption, and implementation. A recent biography, Wallace Ohrt's *Defiant Peacemaker: Nicholas Trist in the Mexican War* (1997), supplements older works on the U.S. diplomat. Dean B. Mahin, *Olive Branch and Sword: The United States and Mexico, 1845–1848* (1997), chronicles the attempts at peacemaking throughout the conflict.

Texas's postannexation experience has received some attention, although there is room for more. Three authors in particular have chronicled Texas's military involvement in the Mexican War: Henry W. Barton, *Texas Volunteers in the Mexican War* (1970); Frederick Wilkins, *The Highly Irregular Irregulars: Texas Rangers in the Mexican War* (1990); and Charles D. Spurlin, *Texas Volunteers in the Mexican War* (1998). The debate over Texas's boundaries is the subject of Mark J. Stegmaier's *Texas, New Mexico, and the Compromise of 1850* (1996). Donald S. Frazier's *Blood and Treasure: Confederate Empire in the Southwest* (1995) describes how Texans unsuccessfully attempted to revive their hopes for territorial acquisition and serves as an epilogue to the three-way struggle between the United States, Texas, and Mexico.

Many important documents relating to this historical period have been published. The following collections are available in libraries: Milo Milton Quaife, ed., *The Diary of James K. Polk during His*

Presidency, 1845–1849 (1910); Moses Austin's *The Austin Papers*, 3 vols., edited by Eugene C. Barker (1924–28); *The Papers of Mirabeau Buonaparte Lamar*, 6 vols. (1921–1927); Amelia W. Williams and Eugene C. Barker, eds., *The Writings of Sam Houston*, 8 vols. (1938–1943); Madge Thornall Roberts, ed., *The Personal Correspondence of Sam Houston*, 4 vols. (1996–2001); and John H. Jenkins, ed., *The Papers of the Texas Revolution, 1835–1836*, 10 vols. (1973).

No story is complete that does not attempt to blend accounts from all sides of the conflicts. The following works will be of great help to students and general readers who want to learn more about the history of Mexico during this period: Michael P. Costeloe, *La primera república federal de México, 1824–1835* (1975); Stanley C. Green, *The Mexican Republic: The First Decade, 1823–1832* (1987); Michael P. Costeloe, *The Central Republic in Mexico, 1835–1846: Hombres de Bien in the Age of Santa Anna* (1993); Timothy E. Anna, *Forging Mexico, 1821–1835* (1998); and Pedro Santoni, *Mexicans at Arms: Puro Federalists and the Politics of War, 1845–1848* (1996). Several authors have attempted studies of Santa Anna, all with varying degrees of success owing to the difficulty of their task, but to date none has done better than Wilfrid Hardy Callcott in *Santa Anna: The Story of an Enigma Who Was Once Mexico* (1936). Margaret Swett Henson's biography of the first vice president of the Republic of Texas, *Lorenzo de Zavala: The Pragmatic Idealist* (1996), reveals much about his role in shaping Mexico's first republican government. An important work that chronicles events in Mexico's northern Mexico during this period is David J. Weber's *The Mexican Frontier, 1821–1846* (1982).

Those looking for information on the Mexican military should see William A. DePalo's *The Mexican National Army, 1822–1852* (1997). An excellent social history of Mexico during this period is *Life in Mexico under Santa Anna, 1822–1855* (1991) by Ruth R. Olivera and Liliane Crété. A work that presents a broad overview of U.S.–Mexican relations is *The United States and Mexico* (1985) by Josefina Zoraida Vásquez and Lorenzo Meyer. The most useful book that I have found for understanding Mexico's attitudes and response toward its aggressive northern neighbor is Gene M. Brack's *Mexico Views Manifest Destiny, 1821–1846* (1975).

Some English-language versions of firsthand Mexican accounts are available. An excellent glimpse of Mexican Texas can be found in *Texas by Terán: The Diary Kept by General Manuel de Mier y Terán on His*

1828 Inspection of Texas (2000), edited by Jack Jackson. *The Mexican Side of the Texan Revolution* (1928) combines the writing of several of its chief participants: Antonio López de Santa Anna, Ramón Martínez Caro, Vicente Filisola, José Urrea, and José María Tornel y Mendivil.

Wallace Woolsey edited General Vincente Filisola's account of the revolution in *Memoirs for the History of the War in Texas*, 2 vols. (1985 and 1987). José Enrique de la Peña's *With Santa Anna in Texas: A Personal Narrative of the Revolution* (1997), edited by Carmen Perry, provides readers with another view of the Texas campaign as seen by a Mexican officer. Santa Anna's perspective can be found in his autobiography, *The Eagle* (1967), edited by Ann Fears Crawford.

Students and others looking for Mexican sources in the post-revolution period will find fewer offerings. Two that are available are *The Second Mexican-Texas War, 1841–1843* (1972) by Miguel. A. Sanchez Lamego and *The Other Side: or Notes for the History of the War between Mexico and the United States* (1850). The second work was written at the end of the Mexican War by a coalition of Mexican scholars and was translated into English by Albert C. Ramsey, an American officer serving in Mexico City.

Several reference works will supply quick answers for students and others. The Texas State Historical Association's (TSHA) six-volume set entitled *The New Handbook of Texas* (1996) contains brief summaries of many of the people and events of this period. TSHA has placed this massive encyclopedia on the Internet, where it is free to all who have access to a computer. The Web address is *http://www.tsha.utexas.edu/handbook/online*. A single-volume treatment of the 3-way relationship between the United States, Mexico, and Texas is *The United States and Mexico at War: Nineteenth-Century Expansionism and Conflict* (1998). The work's editorial board included Donald S. Frazier, Richard B. Winders, Sam W. Haynes, Paul D. Lack, and Pedro Santoni. This book contains articles contributed by many well-known U.S. and Mexican scholars.

INDEX

Boldface page numbers indicate maps; italic page numbers indicate biographical sketches.